3000 YEARS OF BLACK POETRY

3000 YEARS OF BLACK POETRY

An Anthology Edited by

ALAN LOMAX and RAOUL ABDUL

DODD, MEAD & COMPANY · NEW YORK

Second Printing

Library of Congress Catalog Card Number: 76–95909
Printed in the United States of America
by The Cornwall Press, Inc., Cornwall, N.Y.

Thanks are due to the following for permission to reprint the material indicated: Raoul Abdul (translator): for "Call to Prayer," "Humorous Verse," "Prayer to God," "I Vision God," "Love," "Precious Things" from the Raoul Abdul Collection. The North Buxton Folk Museum, North Buxton, Ontario, Canada. Samuel Allen: for "To Satch." Atheneum Publishers: for "On The Appeal From the Race of Sheba II" from SELECTED POEMS BY LEOPOLD SEDAR SENGHOR. English translation by John Reed and Clive Wake, Copyright © 1964 by Oxford University Press. Association for the Study of Negro Life and History: for excerpt from "Les Salazennes" by Auguste Lacaussade (translated by Mercer Cook), "Human Soul" by René Maran (translated by Mercer Cook) from FIVE FRENCH NEGRO POETS (1943). Atlantic Monthly: for "We Delighted, My Friend" by Leopold Sedar Senghor (translated by Miriam Koshland), Copyright © 1959 by the Atlantic Monthly Company, Boston, Mass. Julian Bond: for "Look at That Gal. . . ." Kwesi Brew: for "Lonely Traveler." Broadside Press: for "For Saundra" from BLACK JUDGEMENT by Nikki Giovanni, Copyright © 1968 by Nikki Giovanni. Sterling Brown: for "Strange Legacies," "Strong Men," "Old Lem." Cambridge University Press: for "How Death Came" from HOTTENTOT FABLES AND TALES (1964) by W.H.I. Bleek. "Pretences" (Ibn Rashiq), "The Sword" (Abu Bakr), "The Preacher" (Al-Mahdi), "The Oranges" (Abu Dharr), "Bubbling Wine" (Abu Zakariya) from MOORISH POETRY by A.J. Arberry; "Song for the Sun that Disappeared Behind the Rainclouds," "Death as a Lotus Flower," "The Bird Catcher," "The Sweetest Thing," "The Sky," "Prayer to the God Thot" from AFRICAN POETRY, edited by Ulli Beier. Clarendon Press, Oxford: for "An Elders Reproof to His Wife" (Abdillaahi Muuse), "The Limits of Submission" (Faarh Nuur), "Twelve Modern Love Songs"—English translation only—from pp. 102-4; 134-6; 144-8 of SOMALI POETRY by B.W. Andrezjewski and I.M. Lewis. Collier Books, Inc.: for "Preface to a Twenty Volume Suicide Note" by LeRoi Jones, Copyright © 1961 by LeRoi Jones. "Black Woman," "He Who Has Lost All," "Breaths" translated by Anne Atik from AFRICAN HERITAGE by Jacob Drachler. Waring Cuney: for "My Lord What a Morning," "No Images." Pierre Dalcour: for "Verse Written in the Album of Mademoiselle—." Roland Dempster: for "Africa's Plea" from SONG OUT OF AFRICA, published as a souvenir of the Tubman-Tolbert inauguration, Monrovia, Libya, January 4, 1960. Owen Dodson: for "Confession Stone" from BEYOND THE BLUES by Owen Dodson. Dodd, Mead & Company, Inc.: for "We Wear the Mask" by Paul Laurence Dunbar from THE COMPLETE POEMS OF PAUL LAURENCE DUNBAR. Doubleday Publishing Company, Inc.: for "Hyena," "The Train" from TECHNICIANS OF THE SACRED by Jerome Rothenberg (1968). *Drum Magazine:* for "Pass Office Song" (translated by Peggy Rutherford), "Nativity" by Aquah Laluah. Editions Seghers, Paris: for "Dry Your Tears Africa," "I Give You Thanks My God," "Piano and Drums" by Bernard Dadié from WEST AFRICAN VERSE by Donatus Ibe Nwoga. Estate of Max Eastman: for "Message to Siberia" by A.S. Pushkin (translated by Max Eastman) from THE POEMS, PROSE AND PLAYS OF PUSHKIN, selected and edited by Abraham Yarmolinsky (1936). Halim El-Dahb (translator): for "I Am a Negro" by Muhammad Al-Fituri, "The Potter," "Prelude to Akwasidas." Mari Evans: for "Where Have You Gone?" from NEW NEGRO POETS: U.S.A., edited by Langston Hughes. Exposition Press, Inc., Jericho, New York: for "Harlem" by Jean Brierre from EBONY RHYTHM, edited by Beatrice M. Murphy. Faber and Faber Limited: for "My Thirty Years" by Juan Fransico Manzano (English translation) from A HISTORY OF NEO-AFRICAN LITERATURE by Janheinz Jahn, translated by Oliver Cobarn and Ursula Lehrburger. Farrar, Straus & Giroux, Inc.: for excerpt from "A Sea-Chantey," "Man O' War Bird," "The Whale, His Bulwark," "Nearing La Guaria," "A Far Cry From Africa" by Derek Walcott from SELECTED POEMS BY DEREK

v]   ACKNOWLEDGMENTS

WALCOTT, Copyright © 1962, 1963, 1964 by Derek Walcott. Carol Freeman: for "Christ-
mas Morning I." Fybate Lecture Notes (May 24, 1967) Berkeley, California: for
"Nocturne," by Roussan Camille, "They Came This Evening," "Put Down" by Léon
Damas from BLACK POETRY OF THE FRENCH ANTILLES (translated by Seth L. Wolitz).
Nicolás Guillén: for "Proposition." "Dead Soldier," "Sightseers in a Courtyard." Bobb
Hamilton: for "Poem to a Nigger Cop." Francis Harper: for "The Slave Auction." Harper
and Row, Inc.: for "The Bean Eaters," "We Real Cool" by Gwendolyn Brooks from
SELECTED POEMS, Copyright © 1959 by Gwendolyn Brooks; "Malcolm X" from IN THE
MECCA by Gwendolyn Brooks, Copyright © 1967 by Gwendolyn Brooks. "Heritage,"
"For a Poet," "Yet Do I Marvel," "Simon the Cyrenian Speaks" from ON THESE I STAND
by Countee Cullen, Copyright © 1925 by Harper and Brothers; renewed 1953 by Ida M.
Cullen, "The Lady of the Pearls" (English translation) by Alexandre Dumas Fils from
THE TITANS by André Maurois, translated from the French by Gerald Manley Hopkins,
Copyright © 1957 by André Maurois. Harvey House, Inc. and the Evelyn Singer Agency:
for "Simple Verses" by José Martí from SPANISH AMERICAN POETRY: A BILINGUAL
SELECTION BY SEYMOUR RESNICK, Copyright © 1964 by Harvey House, Inc. Hill and
Wang: for "The Truth," "It's Curtains" by Ted Joans from BLACK POW-WOW, Copy-
right © 1969 by Ted Joans. Mona Hinton (translator): for "Two Countries." Anselm
Hollo (translator): for "Song of the Poor Man," from NEGRO VERSE by Anselm Hollo.
Frank Horne: for "On Seeing Two Brown Boys in a Catholic Church." Yusef Iman: for
"Love Your Enemy." Indiana University Press: for "Shaka, King of the Zulus" (trans-
lated by A.C. Jordan), "Where the Rainbow Ends" by Richard Rive, "Who Knows" by
Milner Brown, "Trousers of Wind" (translated by Slyvia Pankhurst, assisted by Ato
Menghestu Lemme), "Hunger," "The Vultures" by David Diop (translated by Ulli
Beier); first printed in Black Orpheus, from POEMS OF BLACK AFRICA, edited by Langston
Hughes, Copyright © 1963 by Langston Hughes, "Aspiration," "Rondeau for You" by
Mario Andrade (translated by John Nist), "The Words Will Resurrect," "Papa John" by
Jorge de Lima from MODERN BRAZILLIAN POETRY, translated and edited by John Nist.
"Award" by Ray Durem, "The Distant Drum" by Calvin Hernton, "The Pale Blue
Casket" by Oliver Pitcher from NEW NEGRO POETS: U.S.A., edited by Langston Hughes.
International Publishers, Inc.: for "Beginning of a Long Poem on Why I Burned the
City" by Laurence Benford from THE NEW BLACK POETRY. Georgia Douglas Johnson: for
"Common Dust," "Interracial." Fenton Johnson: for "Tired." Joseph Kariuki: for "New
Life." Liveright Publishing Corp.: for "Beehive" from CANE by Jean Toomer, Copy-
right © 1951 by Jean Toomer. Mrs. Coretta King: for "I Have a Dream." Juan Latino:
for "Austriad." Longmans, Green and Company, Ltd.: for "Oriki Erinle," "Shango I,"
"Shango II," "Rumba" from Black Orpheus, edited by Ulli Beier, "Cannibal Hymn"
from THE PYRAMID TEXTS AND COMMENTARY (1952). The Sterling Lord Agency: for
"Audobon Drafted" from THE DEAD LECTURER by LeRoi Jones, published by Grove
Press, Copyright © 1961 by LeRoi Jones. Anna Lomax (translator): for "Who I Am."
Patrice Lumumba: for "Dawn in the Heart of Africa." The Macmillan Company: for
"Mu' Allakat of Antar" from THE SEVEN ODES: THE FIRST CHAPTER IN ARABIC LITERA-
TURE by A.J. Arberry. Agnes Maxwell-Hall: for "Jamaica Market." Mbari Publications:
for "Telephone Conversation" by Wole Soyinka, "Melting Pot" by Michael Echeruo
from Black Orpheus; "Rediscovery" from REDISCOVERY by George Awoonor-Williams,
"After They Put Down Their Overalls" by Lenrie Peters, "The Scorner" by Tchicaya U
Tam'si (translated by Gerald Moore and Ulli Beier). The Morija Sesuto Book Depot,
South Africa: for "The Birth of Mosesh" (Tlhaho Ea Moshoeshoe) translated by David
Cranmer Theko Bereng from LITHOTHOKISO TSA MOSHOESHOE LE TSE LING. The Mosher
Press: for "Farewell" by Isaac Toussaint L' Ouverture, "The Peasant Declares His Love,"
"A Black Girl Goes By" by Emile Roumer, "The Black Man's Son" by Oswald Durand
from THE POETS OF HAITI (translated by Edna Worthley Underwood, 1934). Ezekiel
Mphahlele: for "Autobiography" by Mbella Sonne Dipoko, "Burial" by Paul Joachim
(translated by Oliver Bernard), "Poem of the Conscripted Warrior" by Rui Nogar, "Ap-
peal" by Noemia de Sousa. "Woman" by Valente Goenha Malagatana, "Poem of the
Future Citizen" by José Craveirinha. New Directions Publishing Corp.: for "Battle Re-
port," "Unholy Missions" from SOLITUDES CROWDED WITH LONELINESS by Bob Kaufman,
Copyright © 1965 by Bob Kaufman; "Guinea" by Jacques Roumain, "Training" by
Demetrio S. Herrera (translated by Dudley Fitts) from AN ANTHOLOGY OF LATIN AMERI-
CAN POETRY, edited by Dudley Fitts. Harold Ober Associates, Inc.: for "Southern
Mansion" by Arna Bontemps, Copyright © 1963 by Arna Bontemps; "Without Benefit
of Declaration" by Langston Hughes from AMERICAN NEGRO POETRY, published by Hill
and Wang, Coyright © 1965 by Langston Hughes, "Harlem Sweeties" by Langston
Hughes from SHAKESPEARE IN HARLEM, Copyright © 1942 by Alfred A. Knopf, Inc.;
"Epigram" by Armand Lanusse (translated by Langston Hughes) from THE POETRY

OF THE NEGRO, edited by Langston Hughes and Arna Bontemps, published by Double-day, Copyright © 1949. October House: for "Frederick Douglass" from SELECTED POEMS OF ROBERT HAYDEN, Copyright © 1966 by Robert Hayden. David Okara: for "Mystic Drum," "Piano and Drums." Oxford University Press: for "A Dispute Over Suicide" (translated by T. Eric Peet) from A COMPARATIVE STUDY OF THE LITERATURE OF EGYPT, PALESTINE AND MESOPATAMIA by T. Eric Peet (1931), pp. 115-117 (for the British Academy); "Blue Fly" by Joaquim Maria Machado de Assis (translated by Frances Ellen Buckland), excerpt from "Song of Exile" (translated by Frances Ellen Buckland) from THE EPIC OF LATIN AMERICAN POETRY by Arturo Torres-Rioseco (1942). Regino Pedroso: for "Opinions of a New Student." Pierre-Jean Oswald, Paris: for "Where are These Men Seized in This Wind" by Aldo Do Espirito Santo, "Hidesong" by Aig Higo, "Monamgamba" by Antonio Jacinto from MODERN POETRY OF AFRICA by Ulli Beier and Gerald Moore. Presence Africaine: for extracts from "Return to My Native Land" by Aimé Césaire (translated by Emile Snyders), published in Presence Africaine, Paris (1968), "Fantasy Under the Moon" by Emmanuel Boundzeki-Dongala from Presence Africaine, "Rumba" by José Tallet, "Africa" (Afrique) from COUPS DE PILON, by David Diop, Paris, 1956. M. Flavien Ranaivo: for "Song of a Common Lover." Random House, Inc./Alfred A. Knopf, Inc.: for "Angola Question Mark" from THE PANTHAR AND THE LASH by Langston Hughes, Copyright © 1967 by Arna Bontemps and George Huston Bass, by permission of Alfred A. Knopf, Inc. "The Negro Speaks of Rivers," "When Sue Wears Red," "Mother and Son" from SELECTED POEMS by Langston Hughes, Copyright © 1926 by Alfred A. Knopf, Inc. and renewed 1954 by Langston Hughes. "Trumpet Player" from SELECTED POEMS by Langston Hughes, Copyright © 1947 by Langston Hughes, by permission of Alfred A. Knopf, Inc. "With Freedoms Seed" by Alexander Pushkin (translated by Babette Duetsch) from THE POEMS, PROSE AND PLAYS OF ALEXANDER PUSHKIN, Copyright © 1936 and renewed 1964 by Random House, Inc. "today is a day of great joy" from SNAPS by Victor Hernandez Cruz, Copyright © 1969 by Victor Hernandez Cruz. M. Gabriel Razafintsambaina, "Les Amis de Rabéarivelo": for "What Invisible Rat" by Jean-Joseph Rabéarivelo. Walter Apolphe Roberts: for "On A Monument to Marti." Studio Vista Limited: for "Guadalupe W.I." from NEGRO VERSE by Anselm Hollo. Sam Duby Sutu: for "Night" from MATHE A NTSI. Transition Ltd.: for "Distances" by Christopher Okigbo, Copyright © by Transition Ltd., 1964. University of Texas Press: for "To Columbus," "Alleluya" from SELECTED POEMS OF RUBÉN DARÍO (translated by Lysander Kemp) 1965. Harold Milton Telemaque: for "Adina." Twayne Publishers, Inc.: for "The Tropics of New York," "If We Must Die," "America" from SELECTED POEMS OF CLAUDE MCKAY: excerpt from "Harlem Gallery" by Melvin B. Tolsom. Vanguard Press, Inc.: for "The Hymn to the Sun" by Pharaoh Akhenaton (translated by J.E. Manchip-White), "Love Song" (My Love is a Lotus Blossom), "Love Song" (The Little Sycamore), "Love Song" (I Passed the Door), "Love Song" (My Loved One is Unique), "Love Song" (untitled) from THE GLORY OF EGYPT by Paul Gayet-Tancrede. Viking Press, Inc.: for "O Black and Un-known Bards" by James Weldon Johnson, Copyright © by Grace Nail Johnson. Wit-wastersrand University Press: for "In the Gold Mines," originally published in 1945 as "Ezinkomponi" in AWAL' EXULA by B.W. Vilhaz (Bantu Treasury 8) and published in translation by Howard Timmins, Cape Town, 1962, as "In the Gold Mines" in ZULU HORIZONS: VILAKAZI POEMS, translated into English by D. McK. Malcolm and F.C. Fried-man. Phillis Wheatley: for "To the Right Honorable William, Earl of Dartmouth," "On Being Brought from Africa to America." World Publishing Company: for "Elephant II," "Death Rites II" by C.M. Bowra from PRIMITIVE SONG. Samir Zoghby (translator): for "Quatrains," "The Knell" by Muhammad Al-Fituri.
"The research on which this book is based was supported in part by a grant from the Public Education program of the Ford Foundation."

TO THE MEMORY OF LANGSTON HUGHES

CONTENTS

Haiti

Louisiana

Cuba

Panama

Trinidad

St. Lucia

Introduction

When the highest god, Mpungu, had set the heavenly bodies and all things living in their places, he made a man and a woman and endowed them with reason. However, these two human beings did not as yet possess *mutima* or heart. Mpungu then prepared to depart to his home. He called all his children together to bid them farewell. One after another, they came— the sun, the moon, the rain and darkness. Only *Mutima* was late. At last Mpungu, the high god, grew tired of waiting and disappeared.

Then came little Mutima, crying out for his father. "He has gone," said the others, "Where we do not know." The small one, Mutima, wept and said, "I long to be with him, and, since he has gone, I will enter into man and through him, I will seek God, my father, from generation to generation."

And so it is that in every child of man there dwells Mutima, a heart that longs for and searches after God.

The legend of Mutima is a key to the spirit and culture of black Africa. Indeed, it seems to me that "heart" rather than "soul" epitomizes African traditions and black style. "Soul" is too other-worldly, too disembodied, too fleshless, too Greek, too Presbyterian a term to characterize black creativity. All the poets and singers in this volume have "heart." They are at home not only with themselves, but with everything they see and feel. The real world delights and enchants them. Night and women and love embrace them. The painful follies and ironies of life they totally accept. Besides they feel quite at home with death because, for them, no one has ever died; their ancestors still live, close at hand and beloved. So the quick and the dead, man and nature are made one by *mutima,* man's longing for oneness with the universe. This emotion touches all these poems and poets with tenderness and unifies the varied poetry of the African peoples.

My own pleasure in working on this book has been the discovery of this bond of feeling, of value and of content which links all black singers across the millenia into one family of art. In the writings of Europe, especially, there is a concern with the unique and the individual. The black poet, however, reaches out to touch and experience things outside himself and so is swept up in the worlds of nature and of society. He does not address himself to nature, but brings it into life and handles it. His poem is a hoe with which he breaks and cultivates the soil of reality. He feels that "When one speaks to a woman, one makes her fertile," and he does this by celebrating her real beauty in a poem.

The principal form in the African poetic tradition is the praise song. One of the earliest poems in the book is a black pharaoh's hymn of praise to the sun, as the creator of all things. This psalm is followed by a terrifying song of praise to the Lord of the Horizon, who swallows and devours everything—all men and all gods. Each of these ancient African hymns enumerates the powers and deeds of a deity who controls the natural order of things. By reciting their poetic names and attributes, the poet summons them into life. Thus in all black Africa, poetry and magic and religion become one for praise songs bring the gods to the dancing floor, there to enter the bodies of their devotees and to take part in the affairs of men. Ogun, the god of war, is lauded as . . .

> . . . Ogun, the fire that sweeps the forest
> Ogun, great chief of robbers
> master of iron, head of warriors
> with 400 wives and 1400 children—
> Ogun's laughter is no joke.

The praise song forms compounds a series of formal attributes and honorific titles, each one of which alludes to a myth which all the hearers know, but whose significance would be opaque to a noninitiate. A Yoruba bard praises his King in such terms . . .

. . . however small the needle, the hen cannot swallow it . . .
the toad jumps about happily in the face of the cook . . .
200 needles do not equal a hoe, 200 stars do not make a moon . . .
a good rider will not be thrown off his horse . . .

The singer is telling his listeners in this *oriki* that the enemy can no more overcome their king than a hen can swallow a needle or a cook a toad. Just as 200 needles are no match for a hoe and 200 stars will not make a moon, so 200 men will be no match for the king, and it will be just as impossible to dethrone him as for a horse to throw a good rider.

Unconsciously the poets of the whole black heritage have echoed this praise song style. Rubén Darío, father of modern Latin American literature writes of his mistress . . .

Nests in the warm trees,
eggs in the warm nests,
devotion. Happiness!
The kiss of this blonde girl
and of this tawny girl
and of this black girl.
Happiness!

It is the very heart of the blues . . .

Yonder goes the train, red-blue light behind,
Red for trouble, blue for the worried mind.

Gwendolyn Brooks wrote a praise song for Malcolm X:

He had the hawk man's eyes,
We gasped. We saw the maleness,
Maleness raking out and making guttural the air
And pushing us to the walls.

It was Senghor's superb praise songs to things African that
began the African literary renaissance:

... Naked woman, dark woman!
Heaven-leased gazelle, pearls are stars on the night of your skin,
Delights of the spirit at play
red-gold reflects on your shimmering skin.
In the shade of your hair my anguish lightens with the nearing
    suns of your eyes.
Naked woman, black woman!

The praise song style runs through African tradition from
the Nile to the Mississippi. In it the words do not stand for,
but *are* natural and human things. But this style was not
invented by court poets for kings. It is the essence of African
folk poetry. The Pigmy hunter of Gabon calls the elephant
"the meat that walks like a hill." Far to the west, the Yoruba
hunter says of the elephant, "Wherever he walks, the grass is
forbidden to stand up again."
Sleep, sings the Susu singer,

... is sweeter than honey,
it is sweeter than salt,
it is sweeter than sugar,
it is sweeter than all
existing things.

A verse about death, inscribed on a pyramid, has the same
immediacy...

Death is in my eyes today.
Like the desire of a man to see his home
when he hath passed many years in captivity.

African religion humanizes death, itself. The African believes the land of the dead is all around him, inhabited by ancestors who watch over him and constantly return to feast and dance with him. His poetry becomes the praise of things as they are, of the continual ebb and flow of life—of birth and death, of planting and harvest, of male and female. This African singer, this man of gardens and herds, praises women. In the words of an ageless black proverb, "Women are like God because they bring us children." For him the central values are the erotic, the procreative, the social, and it is this total acceptance of life which gives this collection of verse—drawn from so many languages and across the span of 50 centuries an unexpected unity. At times I have felt that all these pages might have been written by one hand, that all these poems were like so many rapids, so many quiet pools and ripples in the course of an eternal Congo of feeling, of *mutima*, of heart.

The unities and continuities of African style are based, of course, in its cultural patterns. Africa has been a continent preeminent in music, dance, and song. There bards are heroes, and every event of life might be accompanied by song and acted out in dance. Traditional African poetry was sung to melodies of one or two phrase structures, endlessly varied as the singer piles image upon image in the praise song vein. There are other patterns that quicken the music of the whole continent. African poetry has, until recently, always been chanted or sung. Only recently did it lose part of its life on the printed page. Its truest modern practitioners have tried to marry it again to the drum. Therefore, throughout what follows, the history of the black poetic tradition will be linked to music, and much of what is said will be accounted for by reference to song style. It should be added that all the traits attributed to African song and culture are those that have been shown, in the course of a seven-year comparative study of world song style, to be distinctive for Africa.*

African singers tend to use a playful vocal attack, not restraining their voices within one register and one role, but freeing the singer to leap registers, to shift roles, and to use any vocal quality—harsh or placatory—as he chooses. This passionate vocal attack is matched in dance, where outbursts of energy are succeeded by relaxation—and in the poetry as well, where sudden contrasts of mood and image heighten the ironic, angry, or erotic feeling.

The most pervasive and distinctive African musical trait is hot rhythm, which plays through the orchestral music of the primitive hunters, the Bantu gardeners, and the nomads of the Sahara. Hot rhythm, or polymeter, means that two or more contrastive meters, two directions, two moods—one male, one female—are at work within the same musical framework, pulling against one another in combination and in conflict. This sexually freighted rhythmic style not only characterizes most African music, but, because African poetry is sung, it shapes the African tradition from the songs of the black Arab, Antar, to those of LeRoi Jones. Recently the "hot" strain has entered Europe through jazz and the syncopated poetry of Senghor and Guillén.

Beyond this regional unity, there are two clear and distinctive regions of culture, of song and poetry, in Africa—the Mediterranean and Saharan North, and the black South. The North, from Arabia through Egypt and across the Sahara to Morocco, is the land of the solo bard, who addresses the king, the distant god, or the unattainable loved one in a voice of anguish and supplication. This is a world of caste, class, poverty, untrammeled power of lord over vassal, father over children, and husband over wife. Its melodies are heavily embellished with ornaments like sobs, its rhythms are

---

* A complete statement about African musical style in its world setting is contained in *Folk Song Style and Culture*, by Alan Lomax and others, published by the American Association for the Advancement of Science, Washington, D.C., 1968.

slow and often uncertain—the voicing narrow, nasal, tense, and wailing—the mood of the poetry one of despair and long-ing. This high lonesome style shapes the virtuosic poetry of North Africa and penetrates the South wherever Arab culture reaches.

Black African culture fosters strong and forthcoming tem-perament in its women, as well as in its men, and is so posi-tive in regard to procreation that it trains the young in sexual competence. Likewise African song style generally involves women as well as men, is full of erotic symbols, and incites the African chorus to overlap its responses to the leader's part. Africans usually sing in harmony and in polyrhythm. Thus the intent and the effect of this black performance style is erotic—in the most universal sense of that word—that is, to touch and involve all present in a unifying act. This stylistic continuity binds together the songs of Congo pad-dlers, of Zulu storytellers, of West Indian voodooists, of black Baptists, and of freedom marchers. It is also the animating source of black poetic style, for, as the poets of *nègritude* and of the black American renaissance agree, poetry should be sung, experienced, and lived, if it is to have heart (or soul).

Pharaoh Ahkenaton, in the first known poem by a black author, praises the sun as the giver of all life, in a magnificent hymn that is precursor to the psalms of David. The verse of Antar, the black knight of the Arabian desert, expressed ten-der concern for women and so his *Romance* became the source for the tradition of chivalric love which helped to woo Europe away from barbarism. The work of Pushkin, Dumas, of Darío, de Assis, Walcott, MacKay, Hughes, Senghor are alike in concern with love and justice in the real world and in the present. The majority of African poets have been revo-lutionaries and men of action, whose poetry was a statement of their commitment. Today this link between song and deed grows, as black writers see that a runaway geopolitical sys-tem, insensitive to any but its own needs, tries to silence all

voices but its own, in Africa and everywhere—and thus puts
the human continuity, itself, in question. The great Martini-
quean poet, Césaire, cries out against this:

> *And we are standing now, my country and I, hair in the wind,*
> *my little hand now in its enormous fist, and force is not in*
> *us, but above us, in a voice which pierces the night and the*
> *audience like the sting of an apocalyptic hornet.*
> *And the voice declares that for centuries Europe has stuffed*
> *us with lies and bloated us with pestilence,*
> *for it is not true that the work of man is finished*
> *that we have nothing to do in the world*
> *that we are parasites in the world*
> *that we have only to accept the way of the world*
> *but the work of man has only begun*
>
> *and it remains for man to conquer all prohibitions immobilized*
> *in the corners of his fervor*
> *and no race has a monopoly of beauty, intelligence, strength*
>
> *and there is room for all at the rendezvous of conquest and*
> *we know that the sun turns around our earth, lighting only the*
> *portion that our single will has fixed and that every star falls*
> *from sky to earth at our limitless command . . .*

PRIMITIVE SONG

The first human songs may be African, for Africa is the continent where the most ancient human remains have been found alongside the ashes of the first campfires. Remnants of an aboriginal population, the Bushmen and Pigmy hunters, hidden away in isolated pockets of desert and jungle, share a song style whose antiquity matches their way of life. These little people have no chiefs or kings, no permanent habitations. All property is shared. They are pacifists and total egalitarians, their communities being held together by human need alone—and by music. Any one in a Pigmy band may begin the song while all present contribute an independent part. Thus their songs are improvised and superb in complex counterpoint. In fact these little African hunters may have been the inventors of both counterpoint and polyrhythm in the dawn of African time.

Even on this most musical of continents the Pygmies were the acknowledged masters of song and dance. In ancient days they were brought to Egypt to etertain the pharaohs. Truly their songs, with which this anthology begins, have enormous sophistication. In them we encounter, at the beginning of African time, a ripened and mature style, a mood of cool wisdom . . .

The sun gathers up the stars, like a woman collects lizards
Moon splits the hare's lip in anger
Death is a great cold
The elephant frightens the forest

Because of the black habit of setting so much of life's activity to music, Africa is the continent preeminent of song. There is space here for only a few verses from her vast ocean of oral poetry. Yet these fragments will serve to indicate striking similarities between the oral and the written poetry of black Africa. The unabashed, clear, yet passionate view of life, so typical of African written poetry, also characterizes these folk songs, which are no less subtle than the written verse. If they are briefer, this may be because their singers were more concerned with dancing and singing together than in proving their virtuosity.

Sleep conquers millions . . .
There are no accidents in the sky . . .
The hyena is a darkness walker . . .
The elephants forbid the grass to stand . . .
God kills money with a big stick . . .

Gabon Pigmy

DEATH RITES II

The animal runs, it passes, it dies. And it is the great cold.
It is the great cold of the night, it is the dark.
The bird flies, it passes, it dies. And it is the great cold.
It is the great cold of the night, it is the dark.
The fish flees, it passes, it dies. And it is the great cold.
It is the great cold of the night, it is the dark.
Man eats & sleeps. He dies. And it is the great cold.
It is the great cold of the night, it is the dark.
There is light in the sky, the eyes are extinguished,
the star shines.

The cold is below, the light is on high.
The man has passed, the shade has vanished, the prisoner
is free!

Khvum, Khvum, come in answer to our call!
trans: C. M. Bowra

THE ELEPHANT II

Elephant hunter, take your bow!
Elephant hunter, take your bow!

In the weeping forest, under the wing of the evening
the night all black has gone to rest happy:
in the sky the stars have fled trembling,
fireflies shine vaguely and put out their lights:
above us the moon is dark, its white light is put out.
The spirits are wandering.

Elephant hunter, take your bow!
Elephant hunter, take your bow!

In the frightened forest the tree sleeps, the leaves
    are dead,
the monkeys have closed their eyes, hanging from the
    branches above us:
the antelopes slip past with silent steps,
eat the fresh grass, prick their ears,
lift their heads and listen frightened:
the cicada is silent, stops his grinding song.

Elephant hunter, take your bow!
Elephant hunter, take your bow!

In the forest lashed by the great rain
Father elephant walks heavily, *baou, baou,*
careless, without fear, sure of his strength,
Father elephant, whom no one can vanquish:
among the trees which he breaks he stops and starts again:
he eats, roars, overturns trees and seeks his mate:
Father elephant, you have been heard from far.

Elephant hunter, take your bow!
Elephant hunter, take your bow!

In the forest where no one passes but you,
hunter, lift up your heart, leap and walk:
meat in front of you, the huge piece of meat,
the meat that walks like a hill,
the meat that makes the heart glad,
the meat that we'll roast on our coals,
the meat into which our teeth sink,
the fine red meat and the blood we drink smoking.

Elephant hunter, take your bow!
Elephant hunter, take your bow!

trans: C. M. Bowra

Hottentot

SONG FOR THE SUN THAT DISAPPEARED BEHIND THE RAINCLOUDS

The fire darkens, the wood turns black.
The flame extinguishes, misfortune upon us.
God sets out in search of the sun.
The rainbow sparkles in his hand,
the bow of the divine hunter.
He has heard the lamentations of his children.
He walks along the milky way, he collects the stars.
With quick arms he piles them into a basket,
piles them up with quick arms
like a woman who collects lizards
and piles them into her pot, piles them up
until the pot overflows with lizards,
until the basket overflows with light.

trans: Ulli Beier

HOW DEATH CAME

The Moon, they say, called Mantis,
sent him with life to people saying:
Go to men and tell them this—
  As I die and dying live,
  you too shall die and dying live.
Mantis started, took the word.
Then Hare stopped him by the path,

he said: What, insect, is your errand:
Mantis answered: I am sent by Moon,
by that one, I must say to men—
    As he dies and dying lives
    they too shall die and dying live.
Hare the quick-tongue said to him:
Why run? You are shaky on your legs.
Let me go, I outrun the wind.
Hare ran, he came to men and said:
Moon sent me with this word—
    As I die and dying perish
    you shall die and utterly die.
Hare raced again to Moon,
told him all that he had said to men.
The Moon said dark with anger:
How is it you dared tell them
this thing I never said?
He took up wood, a sharp fire-log,
with one blow in the face
struck down the Hare. He split
the lying Hare's lip to this day.

trans: W. H. I. Bleek

Susu

THE SWEETEST THING

There is in this world something
that surpasses all other things
in sweetness.
It is sweeter than honey,
it is sweeter than salt,
it is sweeter than sugar,
it is sweeter than all
existing things.
This thing is sleep.
When you are conquered by sleep
nothing can ever prevent you,
nothing can stop you from sleeping.
When you are conquered by sleep
and numerous millions arrive,
millions arrive to disturb you,
millions will find you asleep.

trans: Ulli Beier

Ewe

THE SKY

The sky at night is like a big city
where beasts and men abound,
but never once has anyone
killed a fowl or a goat,
and no bear has ever killed a prey.
There are no accidents; there are no losses.
Everything knows its way.

trans: Ulli Beier

Hurutsche

My father came in the darkness
And I left in the darkness
Saying, "I do not walk by moonlight—I'm no scared child."
Hyena, my name is not spoken in the nighttime,
I just might come around,
The prowler, the croucher,
Son of the darkness walker.

trans: George Economou

THE TRAIN

Iron thing coming from Pompi, from the round-house
Where Englishmen smashed their hands on it,
It has no front it has no back.
Rhino Tshukudu going that way.
Rhino Tshukudu no, coming this way.
I'm no greenhorn, I'm a strong, skillful man.
Animal coming from Pompi, from Moretele.
It comes spinning out a spider's web under a cloud of gnats
Moved by the pulling of a teat, animal coming from
                                        Kgoboladiatla
Comes out of the big hole in the mountain, mother of the
                                        great woman,
Coming on iron cords.
I met this woman of the tracks curving her way along
                        the river bank and over the river.

I thought I'd snatch her
So I said
"Out of the way, son of Mokwatsi, who stands there
                                        at the teat."
The stream of little red and white birds gathered up
                                        all of its track
Clean as a whistle.
Tshutshu over the dry plains
Rhino Tshukudu out of the high country
Animal from the south, steaming along
It comes from Pompi, the round-house, from Kgobola-diatla.

trans: D.F. v.d. Merwe

Yoruba

THE ELEPHANT I

Elephant, who brings death.
Elephant, a spirit in the bush.
With a single hand
he can pull two palm trees to the ground.
If he had two hands
he would tear the sky like an old rag.
The spirit who eats dog,
the spirit who eats ram,
the spirit who eats
a whole palm fruit with its thorns.
With his four mortal legs
he tramples down the grass.
Wherever he walks
the grass is forbidden to stand up again.

trans: Gbadamosi & Beier

ORIKI ERINLE

He is firm and strong
like an ancient rock.
He is clear like the eye of god
that does not grow any grass.
Like the earth he will never change.
He puts out the lamp
and lets his eye sparkle like fire.

He will turn the barren woman
into one who carries child.
He is the father of our king.
He is the one who looks after my child.

trans: Ulli Beier

SHANGO I

Shango is the death who kills money with a big stick
The man who lies will die in his home
Shango strikes the one who is stupid
He wrinkles his nose and the liar runs off
Even when he does not fight, we fear him
But when war shines in his eye
His enemies and worshippers run all the same
Fire in the eye, fire in the mouth, fire on the roof
The leopard who killed the sheep and bathed in its blood
The man who died in the market and woke up in the house

trans: Gbadamosi & Beier

SHANGO II

Shango is an animal like the gorilla
A rare animal in the forest
As rare as the monkey who is a medicine man
Shango, do not give me a little of your medicine
Give me all! So that I can spread it over my face & mouth
Anybody who waits for the elephant, waits for death
Anybody who waits for the buffalo, waits for death
Anybody who waits for the railway, waits for trouble
He says we must avoid the thing that will kill us
He says we must avoid trouble
He is the one who waited for the things we are running away
from

trans: Gbadamosi & Beier

Dahomey

SONG FOR THE DEAD, III

I see it,
There is no enjoying beyond Death,
And I say to all of you say,
That which your senses taste of Life
Goes with you.

I say to you say
The wives you have,
The passion you know of them
Goes with you.

I say to you say
The drinks you drink,
The pleasure of them
Goes with you.

I say to you say
The meats you eat,
The relish you have of them
Goes with you.

I say to you say
The pipes you smoke,
The quiet they bring
Goes with you.

Come, then
Dance all the colors of Life
For a lover of pleasure
Now dead.

trans: Frances S. Herskovits

Twi

PRELUDE TO AKWASIDAE

He who saved Ankoma   Oh nature
Born a drummer
Now   This moment
I start again

By nature the drum was made
And by nature I was created
I am a drummer
Once I travelled and was not there
Here   I come again
Born   a drummer

Here I come again
Like the fantum tree
When stabbed and cut   will always heal

Kodia   the drum   ever-present
Kodia Tweneduro speaks before sunrise

Like the funtum tree
The drummer and the drum   ever-present

Rise up   Rise up
In the shadow of dawn
With the sounds of the rooster

Early   Early   Early

Huuuuuuuuuuuuuuuuuuuu—beeeeeeeeeeeeee

NOTE: Akwasidae—a festival paying homage to a chief and pouring libations
     for the gods.
Ankoma—a man's name procted by nature
Funtum—a tree that produces rubber
Kodia—a drum's name
Tweneduro—a drum's title or second name

trans: Halim El-Dabh

Zulu

SHAKA, KING OF THE ZULUS

He is Shaka the unshakable,
Thunderer-while-sitting, son of Menzi.
He is the bird that preys on other birds,
The battle-axe that excels other battle-axes.
He is the long-strided-pursuer, son of Ndaba,
Who pursued the moon and the sun.
He is a great hubbub like the rocks of Nkandla
Where the elephants take shelter
When the heavens frown.
'Tis he whose spears resound causing wailings,
Thus old women shall stay in abandoned homes,
And old men shall drop by the wayside.

trans: A. C. Jordan

South Africa

PASS OFFICE SONG

The scene is any pass office, where all male Africans must go to get their Registration Certificates. There they may wait in queues for hours and sometimes for days before they are attended to. It is a regulation which rankles in their minds and so they sing about it.

Take off your hat.
What is your home name?
Who is your father?
Who is your chief?
Where do you pay your tax?
What river do you drink?
We mourn for our country.

trans: Peggy Rutherford

EGYPT

Europeans, accustomed to seeing the peristyles, the sculpture, and the tombs of Egypt in their museums, tend to think of it as an ancient, if somewhat odd part of their world. But Egypt is African not only in geographic and linguistic terms, but in a cultural and literary sense as well. The southern half of the country in the upper Nile, moreover, is Nubian or Sudanese and, therefore, black. It is quite likely that the upper Nile saw the genesis of Egyptian civilization. Whether this be so or not, trade, conquest, slaving, and migration maintained such constant interflow between northern and southern Egypt that traces of Mediterranean Egypt are found all the way to Tanganyika, and things of black Africa are familiar in Cairo. Little question that, from the beginning, black Africans took a hand in the development of Egyptian civilization, its arts, and its poetry.

That individuals, known to be black and Negro, played important roles in the flowering of ancient Egypt is a fact well known to historians, though seldom mentioned by them. For example, black Imhotep, sometimes called the father of medicine, was so famous a healer in the third millenium that in later times he came to be worshipped as a god.

Folklore then transformed him into the little black bambino of the Roman church.

In the second millenium Thotmes enlarged the Kingdom of Egypt by skilled and ruthless conquests. His sculptured head declares the Negro origin of this mighty general who rose from priesthood to head the Egyptian empire. A far different king was his descendant, Akhenaton, who ascended to the throne in 1372 B.C., like many pharaohs before him, in order to prevent intrigue and to keep the royal line pure, he married his sister, Nephretiti. Her portrait bust, carved in black stone to indicate her race, shows her to be one of the supremely beautiful women of all time.

Akhenaton inherited, as his personal property, the greatest and richest empire any man had ever seen. With his army, he had unchallenged power, but gentle Akhenaton did not care for glory or conquest. He believed and practiced peace and charity. He ordered the chains struck from the slaves of Egypt. He abolished the use of the lash. When vassal nations rebelled, he refused to attack them, saying they could be free. Thirteen hundred years before Christ, Akhenaton preached the gospel of peace, of truth, and of brotherhood. He turned against the pantheistic religion of his forefathers and proclaimed his belief in one god in a hymn of praise that prefigures the Psalms of David. One of Akhenaton's psalms reads:

> O Lord how manifold are Thy works
> The whole land is in joy and holiday because of Thee
> They shout to the height of heaven
> All that Thou hast made leaps before Thee.
> Thou makest the beauty of form through Thyself alone

In these lines, Akhenaton, the earliest known monotheist, "gives," as Breasted says, "the first signal of the religion that the West upholds today. There follows his *Hymn to the Sun*, the first poem known to have been written by a black poet.

THE HYMN TO THE SUN

Beautiful you rise upon the horizon of heaven,
O living sun, you who have existed since the beginning of
things ...
The whole world is filled with your loveliness.
You are the god Ra, and you have brought every land under
your yoke,
Bound them in with the force of your love.
You are far away, yet your beams flood down upon the earth.
You shine upon the faces of men,
And no one is able to fathom the mystery of your coming.

When you sleep in the West, beneath the horizon,
The earth is plunged in a shadow
That resembles the shadow of death.
Then men sleep in their dwellings,
Their heads muffled, their nostrils blocked,
And no one's gaze encounters that of his fellow.
Then robbers steal into houses
And filch the valuables from beneath pillows
And creep away undetected.
The lion pads forth from his lair
And poisonous creatures bare their fangs.
Oh, how dark it is!
And what a brooding silence falls over the world,
When the maker of all things slumbers in the West!

But when the dawn comes you glitter on the horizon ...
When day breaks, you chase away the black shades ...
The Two Lands awake rejoicing,
Men rise up and stand upon their feet
With their arms stretched wide to hail your emergence!
The whole world then begins to go about its business.
The cattle champ their fodder contentedly;
Trees and plants open their leaves,

And birds forsake their nests,
Spreading their wings in adoration of your soul.
The young goats bound upwards,
And everything that flies and flaps its wings
Takes on a new lease of life when you smile upon it.
Boats are able to sail up and down the great river.
Your light illumines the highways and byways.
The very fish in the water cavort before you,
And your beams strike to the very depths of the ocean.

You nourish the germ in a woman's womb
And from the seed make man,
Guarding the child in its mother's womb,
Calming and soothing its tears.
You nurse and feed it before it is born,
You breathe life into the creatures you fashion.
On the day when the child leaves the womb
You open its mouth
And minister to its needs.
The chick inside the egg squeaks in its shell,
For you reach it and bestow upon it your breath
In order to make it live.
You give the tender chick strength to free itself
And to come crowing from the egg,
Standing immediately upon its feet.

Your rays provide nutriment for the fields,
And when you smile, they flourish
And become fruitful for you.
You ordained the seasons
To keep alive your handiwork.
You gave the winter to provide a breathing-space,
And also the summer heat.
You made the distant sky itself,
In order that you could appear resplendent there and look
                                                        down

On the world you had created.
It is you alone who shine forth
In your innumerable aspects,
Whether you are but dimly perceived
Or visible in all your splendour,
Whether you are far or whether you are near.
You have created millions of things,
Towns and cities, fields, rivers and roads.
You are the focus of every eye
When you stand at your glorious zenith.

How numerous are your works,
And how mysterious to our mortal eyes!
You are the only god, you have no peer,
You made the world after your own heart,
And you created it on your own.
You made men and beasts, you made every wild and
                                        domesticated animal,
Everything that lives and moves upon earth,
Everything that spreads its wings and flies in the firmament.
You made the foreign lands of Syria and Nubia,
And you made our own land of Egypt.
You decreed every man's tasks and status
And made provision for their requirements.
You allotted to everyone his livelihood and span of life.
You ordained the diverse tongues in which the peoples speak,
Their peculiar character
And their different colourings.
You gave individuality to the various geographical regions.
You made the Nile spring from the Lower World
And gush forth lovingly
To nurture the inhabitants of our land,
Who belong to you,
Their Lord, because of your loving kindness towards them.

O Master of all lands,
You shine out above them,
Day-Sun, mighty in power;
You have brought life to the most distant countries,
And given them a Heavenly Nile
To shed its waters upon them,
To inundate their slopes with its ripples,
To irrigate the fields between their villages.
All the mortals who have been on earth
Since the beginning of time
Have been brought up to honour your son, issue of your
flesh,

Pharaoh of the Two Egypts,
Who dwells with Truth . . .
Whose lifetime is long;
And also in honour of his revered royal wife, whom Pharaoh
loves,

Mistress of the Two Lands,
The Queen who lives and flourishes
For ever and ever.

trans: J. E. Manchip White

THE CANNIBAL HYMN

The sky is heavy, it is raining stars.
The arches of the sky are cracking; the bones of the
earthgod tremble;
The Pleiades are struck dumb by the sight of Unas
Who rises towards the sky, transfigured like a god,
Who lives off his father and eats his mother.
He is the bull of the sky; his heart lives off the
divine beings;
He devours their intestines, when their bodies are charged
with magic.
It is he who passes judgment, when the elders
are slaughtered.

He is Lord over all meals.
He ties the sling with which he catches his prey,
He prepares the meal himself.
It is he who eats men and lives off the gods.
He has servants who execute his orders.
Skullgrabber catches them for him, like bulls with a lasso.
Headerect watches them for him and brings them to him;
Willow-croucher binds them
And tears their intestines from their body;
Winepresser slaughters them
And cooks a meal for him in his evening pots.
Unas swallows their magic powers.
He relishes their glory.
The large ones among them are his morning meal,
The medium size are his lunch,
The small ones among them he eats for supper.
Their senile men and women he burns as incense.
The great ones in the North sky lay the fire for him
With the bones of the elders,
Who simmer in the cauldrons themselves;
Look, those in the sky work and labor for Unas.
They polish the cookingpots for him with thighs
                                        of their wives.

O Unas has reappeared in the sky,
He is crowned as Lord of the Horizon,
Those he meets in his path he swallows raw.
He has broken the joints of the gods,
Their spines and their vertebrae.
He has taken away their hearts,
He has swallowed the red crown,
He has eaten the green crown,
He feeds on the lungs of the Wise,
He feasts, as he now lives on hearts,
And on the power they contain.
He thrives luxuriously, for all their power is in his belly,

His nobility can no longer be taken away.
He has consumed the brain of every god,
His life time is eternity,
His limit is infinity.

trans: Samuel A. B. Mercer

A DISPUTE OVER SUICIDE

. . . .

To whom should I speak today?
Brothers are evil
the friends of today love not.

To whom should I speak today?
Hearts are covetous
every man plundereth the goods of his fellow.

To whom should I speak today?
Yesterday is forgotten
men do not as they were done by nowadays.

To whom should I speak today?
There is no heart of man
whereon one might lean.

To whom should I speak today?
The righteous are no more
the land is given over to evil-doers.

To whom should I speak today?
There is a lack of companions
men have recourse to a stranger to tell their troubles.

To whom should I speak today?
I am heavy-laden with misery
& without a comforter.

. . . .

Death is in my eyes today
as when a sick man becomes whole
as the walking abroad after illness.

Death is in my eyes today
like the scent of myrrh
like sitting beneath the boat's sail on a breezy day.

Death is in my eyes today
like the smell of water-lilies
like sitting on the bank of drunkenness.

Death is in my eyes today
like a well-trodden road
as when men return home from a foreign campaign.

Death is in my eyes today
like the unveiling of the heaven
as when a man attains to that which he knew not.

Death is in my eyes today
like the desire of a man to see his home
when he hath passed many years in captivity.

trans: T. Eric Peet

DEATH AS A LOTUS FLOWER

I am the pure Lotus,
that blossomed on the horizon,
that grows in the nostril of the sungod.
I am the pure lotus,
that blossomed in the field.

trans: Ulli Beier

LOVE SONG

My love is a lotus blossom,
Her breast is a pomegranate . . .
Her forehead is a snare of meyru-wood,
And I am the wild bird
Tempted by the toothsome trap.

> Thirteenth Century B.C.
> *trans: J. E. Manchip White*

PRAYER TO THE GOD THOT

The tall palm tree sixty feet high
heavy with fruit:
the fruit contains kernels,
the kernels water.
You who bring water to the remotest place

come and save me because I am humble.
O Thot, you are a sweet well
for him who starves in the desert.
A well that remains closed to the talkative

but opens up to the silent.
When the silent man approaches, the well reveals itself;
when the noisy man comes you remain hidden.

> *trans: Ulli Beier*

THE BIRD CATCHER

I have come to catch birds;
I carry my bird net with me,
a trap in one hand
the net and missile in the other.

Look, all the birds of Punt
are descending on Egypt,

scented with myrrh.
The first bird that lands,
fooled by my bait,
is fragrant with the perfume of Punt,
his claws steeped in balm.

This is my desire:
with you to release it,
to be alone with you
when it sounds the call of freedom,
my bird, scented with myrrh.

I know nothing more beautiful
when I set my traps
than to have you with me.
Glorious: to walk across the field
towards my beloved.

trans: Ulli Beier

LOVE SONG

The little sycamore
That she planted with her own hand
Opens its mouth to speak.
Its rustling is as sweet
As a draught of honey.
How beautiful its graceful branches
In their greenness!
On it hang young fruit and fruit that is ripe,
Redder than the blood-red jasper;
Its leaves are the colour of green jasper.

The love of my loved one is on the other shore.
An arm of the river lies between us,
And crocodiles lurk on the sand-banks.
But I enter the water, I plunge into the flood;

My eager heart carries me swiftly over the waves;
I swim as surely as though I were walking
                              on the solid ground.
Love, it is love that gives me strength,
Averting the perils of the river.

Eighteenth Dynasty (1580–1320 B.C.)
trans: J. E. Manchip White

LOVE SONG

I passed by the house of the young man who loves me;
I found the door was open.
He sat at his mother's side,
In the midst of his brothers and sisters.
Everyone who passes in the roadway loves him.
He is a fine young man, a man with no equal,
A lover of rare character.
And how he stared out at me as I passed by the house!
(I was walking abroad on my own, for my own enjoyment.)
And how my heart leaped up with love,
My dearest lover, when I set eyes on you!
Ah! If only my mother knew what was in my heart
She would go and visit him in a flash!
O golden goddess, inspire in her this thought!
Oh, how I wish to go to my love,
To embrace him openly in front of his family,
And weep no longer because of people's attitude,
To be happy because everyone knows at last
That he and I are in love with each other.
I would hold a little festival in honour of my goddess!

My heart is on fire with the idea of venturing abroad again
                                                     tonight
In order to catch another glimpse of my lover . . .

Fourteenth Century B.C.
trans: J. E. Manchip White

LOVE SONG

My loved one is unique, without a peer,
More beautiful than any other.
See, she is like the star that rises on the horizon
At the dawn of an auspicious year.
She moves in a shimmer of perfection, her complexion
                                            superb,

Her eyes are marvellously seductive,
On her lips linger persuasive words.
Never does she speak one word too many!
Her neck is slender, ample her breast,
Her hair is lapis lazuli;
Her arms more splendid than gold
And her fingers like lotus-petals.
Her robe is tightly caught in around her waist,
Revealing the most beautiful legs in all the world . . .
You cannot help following her with your eyes wherever
                                            she goes,

She is such an unrivalled goddess in appearance.

Fourteenth Century B.C.
trans: J. E. Manchip White

LOVE SONG

My boat sails downstream
In time to the strokes of the oarsmen.

A bunch of reeds is on my shoulder,
And I am travelling to Memphis, "Life of the Two Lands."
And I shall say to the god Ptah, Lord of Truth:
"Give me my fair one tonight."
The god Ptah is her tuft of reeds,
The goddess Sekhmet is her posy of blossoms,
The goddess Earit is her budding lotus,
The god Nefertum is her blooming flower.

My love will be happy!
The dawn irradiates her beauty.

Memphis is a crop of pomegranates,
Placed before the god with the handsome countenance.

Nineteenth Dynasty (1320–1200 B.C.)
trans: J. E. Manchip White

BLACK RAVENS

of the Arab World

Arabia lies close to the eastern flank of Africa and throughout history has been linked to it by sea routes and caravan trails. For more than a thousand years the language, religion, and politics of North Africa have been Arab. The ancient caravan routes that crisscrossed the Sahara not only brought Arab culture into the black world, but along them the treasures of black Africa moved North to the Mediterranean world. Like Africans, Arabs compose their verse in praise song vein and sing it to drum accompaniment. Indeed, the chief glory of Arab poetry is in the variety of its complex syncopated meters, which seem to echo the enchantment of African drums.

As in all black Africa, the Bedouins of the desert see the poet as a wizard endowed with magical powers. The foaling of a blooded mare, the birth of a boy, and the coming to light of a poet alike cause general rejoicing. The discovery of a poet in a family brings the whole tribe together to feast its good luck, for a poet defends the honor of a clan and perpetuates its glorious deeds forever. So it is that Arab literary historians do not conceal the racial origin of black writers,

but tenderly refer to them as "our black ravens." All acknowl-
edge the greatest of these black ravens, the slave Antar, as
one of the founders of Arab literature.

Antar's mother was the Abyssinian concubine of a desert
sheik. His father refused to legitimize him until, one day
when the tide of battle had turned against him, the old
sheik called on Antar for help. The young man replied, "I
cannot fight. A slave is only good for milking camels and
binding their udders." "Charge," called the old man. "I declare you a free man." Antar charged and routed the enemy,
singing—

> I am the mongrel Antar!
> Every man defends his woman,
> whether she be black or white,
> whether she be smooth or hairy.

His father endowed him with the name of the lineage.
Then Antar, the ex-slave, became the knightly hero of the
Arab world in the violent dawn of its civilization. "Only
three things are worthy of a man," said this sanguinary poet,
"to make love, to make war, and to make verse." And in the
6th Century the whole Peninsula rang with the deeds of this
wild, black desert rider, whose songs were as thrilling as
his amorous escapades. Indeed, Antar, who was never
troubled by modesty, was his own best biographer. He left
behind him a tremendous romantic poem of which he was
the hero. First printed in Beirut in sixteen volumes, this
gallant history of desert battles and seductions, enshrining
the life style of a black Bedouin knight of the desert, was
carried across Africa and into Spain with the Arab conquest.
The Romance of Antar became the source for the courtly
romances of the Middle Ages, and so, by curious irony, it is
the way of life and love of a black Bedouin that is the model
and source for the European tradition of chivalry and courtly
love. The great French critic, Renan, said of Antar:

. . . if in all the history of civilization there is a picture more graceful, more thrilling than Arab life before Islam, such as we are permitted to look upon it in the magnificent type which was Antar; boundless freedom of the individual, absence of power, law, exalted ideals of honor, a chivalrous grace, airy fancy, the exquisiteness and refinements of love.

Antar died in battle in 615. In 1937, 1300 years later, the Negro poet Claude MacKay was welcomed in the cafés of Marrekesh by: "Mezziane, MacKay! Our greatest poet, Antar, was also black."

Black men stride through the whole of Arabian history. The slave, Bilal, Mohammed's first convert, became Treasurer of Islam and first sang the muezzin call to prayer that still echoes from every minaret in the Moslem world. Black emperors ruled in the Middle East in Egypt, Morocco, and in Spain, among them Ibrahim al-Mahdi, Caliph of Bagdad, and brother of Haroun al-Rashid of the *Arabian Nights*. It was said of Ibrahim that in singing, in rhythm, and in playing the stringed instrument he excelled all men of his time. As caliph of an empire that then stretched from India to Spain, the extravagance of Caliph Ibrahim matched that of his verses. He had a tree of gold with singing golden birds that ran by clockwork. He once tipped a singer the equivalent of $50,000 in silver dirhams. When he forgot to pay his soldiers, they called out, "Since the man cannot pay us, bring him to us and let him sing for us," and they forgave him when they heard him sing. Ibrahim cared more for poetry than for power and he willingly turned over the throne to his rival Mamoun and became the chief singer in the palace where he had occupied the throne.

Men like Ibrahim rode into Spain with the conquering part-Berber, part-black-Sudanese, armies of Morocco. In the cultural centers and in the universities of Moorish Spain a heritage of Greek, Egyptian, Arabic, and African culture came to a new flowering, and it was from these cultural centers that mathematics, philosophy, poetry, and the idea of courtly love lit the fires of the Renaissance in Europe. Meanwhile, in the Arab-speaking world of north Africa—from Morocco to Somaliland and Zanzibar—the complex art of Arabic poetry has continued to flourish. The Arab-speaking Sudanese feel only two occupations are worthy of a gentleman—poetry or politics. Somaliland is a nation of bards where the gift of poetry is one that all covet and many possess. The latest style in Somali verse was created in this decade by a lorry driver.

Arab

ANTAR, warrior poet of the sixth century, is author of the *Mu'allaqa*, which is one of the seven poems written in letters of gold and suspended in the Temple at Mecca. His legend inspired Rimsky-Korsakov to compose the *Antar Symphony* (Opus 9).

THE MU'ALLAQA OF ANTAR

Have the poets left a single spot for a patch to be sewn?
Or did you recognise the abode after long meditation?
O abode of Abla at El-Jawá, let me hear you speak;
I give you good morning, abode of Abla, and greetings to you!
For there I halted my she-camel, huge-bodied as a castle,
that I might satisfy the hankering of a lingerer;
while Abla lodge at El-Jawá, and our folk dwelt
at El-Hazn and Es-Sammán and El-Mutathallim.
All hail to you, ruins of a time long since gone by,
empty and desolate since the day Umm el-Haitham parted.
She alighted in the land of the bellowers; and it has become
very hard for me to seek you out, daughter of Makhram.
Casually I fell in love with her, as I slew her folk
(by your father's life, such a declaration is scarce opportune),
and you have occupied in my heart, make no doubt of it,
the place of one dearly beloved and highly honoured.
But how to visit her, now her people are in spring-quarters
at Unaizatan, while ours are dwelling in El-Ghailam?

If you were resolved upon departing, assuredly
it was a dark night your camels were bridled on;
nothing disquieted me, but that her people's burthen-beasts

were champing khimkhim-berries amid their habitations,
two and forty milch-camels among them, all black
as the inner wing-feathers of the sable raven.
When she captures you with that mouthful of sharp white
                                                            teeth,
sweet indeed the kiss of it, delicious to taste,
you might think a merchant's musk-bag borne in its basket
has outstripped the press of her side-teeth, wafted from her
                                                    mouth to you,
or an untrodden meadow that a good rain has guaranteed
shall bear rich herbage, but sparsely dunged, not known
                                                            of men,
visited by every virgin raincloud bountiful in showers
that have left every puddle gleaming like a silver dirham,
deluging and decanting, so that at every eve
the water is streaming over it in unbroken flow;
and there the fly sits alone, unceasingly
humming away, like a toper raising his voice in song,
trilling, the while he rubs one leg against another
just like a one-armed man bending to strike the flint.
She lolls evening and morning lazily upon a pillow
while I ride through the night on a black, well-bridled mare
with a saddle for my cushion, laid on a stout-legged beast
very large in the flanks, generous in the girth.
Would I indeed be brought to her dwelling by a Shadani
                                                    she-camel
cursed by an udder barren of milk and withered up,
lashing her tail after all night travelling, still a-swagger,
stamping the sand-mounds with pads heavily tramping?
At eventide it is as though I am breaking the hillocks
upon an ostrich close-footed, that lacks for ears,
to which the young ostriches flutter, as herds of
                                                    Yemeni camels
flock to the call of a barbarous, incomprehensible voice;
they follow after the crest of his head; he is like a litter

laid upon a sort of bier, and tented for them,
small-headed, visiting his eggs in Dhul Ushaira,
like an ear-lopped slave swaggering in long furs.
My camel drank of the waters of Ed-Duhrudán
then swerved and fled, avoiding the pools of Ed-Dailam,
as though she twisted her right side to get away
from a big-headed beast that screams at evening,
a cat padding beside her, and every time she turns
to him in anger he wards her off with claws and teeth.
Long journeying has left her with a strong-built back,
high-hoisted, supported on props like a tent-pitcher's.
She knelt down at the waters of Er-Ridá', and you might
                                                  have said
it was upon crackling cleft reeds that she knelt down,
and it was like as if thick butter-fat or molten pitch
that is used to kindle a blaze about a boiler
welled out from the back of the neck of an angry, spirited
proud-stepping she, the match of a well-bitten stallion.

If you should lower your veil before me, what then? Why,
I am a man skilled to seize the well-armoured knight.
Praise me therefore for the things you know of me; for I
am easy to get on with, provided I'm not wronged;
but if I am wronged, then the wrong I do is harsh indeed,
bitter to the palate as the tang of the colocynth.
It may also be mentioned how often I have drunk good wine,
after the noon's sweltering calm, from a bright figured bowl
in a glittering golden glass scored with lines
partnered to a lustrous filtered flask on its left,
and whenever I have drunk, recklessly I squander
my substance, while my honour is abounding, unimpaired,
and whenever I have sobered up, I diminish not my bounty,
my qualities and my nobility being as you have known then.
And many's the good wife's spouse I have left on the floor,
the blood whistling from his ribs like a harelip hissing,

my fists having beaten him to it with a hasty blow
and the spray of a deep thrust, dyed like dragon's blood.
I could advise you, daughter of Malik, to ask the horsemen
if you should happen to be ignorant and uninformed,
for I'm never out of the saddle of a strong swimmer,
sturdy, assaulted again and again by the warriors, wounded,
now detached for the lance-thrusting, and anon
resorting to the great host with their tight bows.
Those who were present at the engagement will acquaint you
how I plunge into battle, but abstain at the booty-sharing.
Many's the bristling knight the warriors have shunned

                                        to take on,

one who was not in a hurry to flee or capitulate,
my hands have been right generous to with the hasty thrust
of a well-tempered, strong-jointed, straightened spear
giving him a broad, double-sided gash, the hiss of which
guides in the night-season the prowling, famished wolves;
I split through his accoutrements with my solid lance
(for even the noblest is not sacrosanct to the spear)
and left him carrion for the wild beasts to pounce on,
all of him, from the crown of his head to his limp wrists.

Many's the time I've ripped with my sword the links of a

                                        long

well-riveted mail-coat off a signal defender of the right;
nimble his hands were with the gaming-arrows in winter,
he tore down traders' inn-signs, and was much chided.
When he beheld me come down in the field against him
he bared his back-teeth, and not in a grin I may say;
so I thrust him with my lance, then I came on top of him
with a trenchant Indian blade of shining steel,
and when the sun was high in the heavens I descried him
his fingers and his head as it were dyed with indigo—
a true hero, as if he were a clothed sarha-tree,
shod in shoes of tanned leather, no weakling twin.

O lovely fawn, huntable indeed for those who may enjoy her
but to me denied—and would to God she were lawful to me—
I sent my slave-girl to her, telling her, "Off with you now,
scout out news of her for me, and tell me truly."
She said, "I saw the enemy were off their guard
and the fawn was attainable to any good marksman."
As she turned, her throat was like a young antelope's,
the throat of a tender gazelle-fawn with spotted upper lip.

I am told that Amr is ungrateful for my beneficence,
and ingratitude is a heaviness to the soul of the benefactor.
I have minded well the counsel my uncle gave me in the
forenoon
when fearfully the lips drew back from the mouth's white
teeth
in the thick of death, of whose agonies the true hero
utters no complaint, other than a muffled cry:
when my comrades thrust me against the lances, I did not
shrink
from them, but my field of advance was narrowly choked.
When in the midst of the battle-dust I heard the cry
of Murra ascend shrill, and the two sons of Rabí'a,
and all Muhallim were striving beneath their banner
and death stalked beneath the sons of Muhallim's banner,
then I knew for sure that when the issue was joined with them
such a blow would fall as to scare the bird from its snuggling
chicks.
When I beheld the people advancing in solid mass
urging each other on, I wheeled on them blamelessly;
"Antara!" they were calling, and the lances were like
well-ropes sinking into the breast of my black steed.
Continuously I charged them with his white-blazoned face
and his breast, until his body was caparisoned in blood,
and he twisted round to the spears' impact upon his breast
and complained to me, sobbing and whimpering;

had he known the art of conversation, he would have
protested,
and had he been acquainted with speech, he would have
spoken to me.
The horses frowning terribly plunged into the crumbling soil,
long-bodied mare along with short-haired, long-bodied
stallion,
and oh, my soul was cured, and its faint sickness was healed
by the horsemen's cry, "Ha, Antara, on with you!"

Submissive are my riding-camels; wherever I will go
my heart accompanies me, and I urge it with firm command.
I greatly feared that death might claim me, before
war's wheel should turn against the two sons of Damdam,
who blaspheme against my honour, and I have not reviled
them,
who threaten to spill my blood, if I do not meet them;
and well they may, it being myself that left their father
carrion for the wild beasts and all the great vultures.

trans: A. J. Arberry

BILAL, a former African slave who lived around 600, was the first man appointed to chant the Muslim *Call to Prayer*. Five times a day, at dawn, at noon, in the afternoon, at sunset and again at night, the citizens of Mecca would hear Bilal's beautiful voice ringing out over the city. So great was Mohammed's admiration of Bilal that on his deathbed the prophet named Bilal as his successor. Bilal yielded in favor of the great general Abu Bekr.

MUHAMMEDAN CALL TO PRAYER
As sung by Bilal

God is the Most High.
I witness that there is none to worship except God.
I witness that Muhammad is the Apostle of God.
Arise to prayer. Arise to divine service.

trans: Raoul Abdul

ABU DOLAMA (d. 778) was an Abyssinian Negro who was court jester to the caliphs Mansur and Mahdi. Once the caliph and his minister Ali ben Suleiman were hunting gazelles. The caliph hit one, but the minister missed and killed a dog instead. Abu Dolama composed a little verse commenting on the event.

HUMOROUS VERSE

The caliph shot a gazelle,
And Ali shot a dog.
Bravo!
Each will eat of the provision he acquired.

trans: Raoul Abdul

Moorish

PRETENCES
by Ibn Rashiq (d. 1064)

What makes me disinclined
To visit Andalus
Is the pretentious kind
Of names their rulers use.

The folly that confers
Great names on little scions
Is like the cat, that purrs
To ape the rage of lions.

trans: A. J. Arberry

THE SWORD
by Abu Bakr (d. 1116)

My sword I shook
Until
It glittered like a brook,
But frozen, still . . .

I watched it glow
As bright
As flaming fire, although
Extinguished quite.

Were it not cold
And dead,
It would have burned, or rolled
Away, I said . . .

trans: A. J. Arberry

THE PREACHER
by Al-Mahdi (d. 1130)

Their shoulders you shook
When they parted; but they
Completely forsook
You, when you went away.

Fine lessons you teach,
But yourself do not school;
Grand sermons you preach,
And remain still a fool.

How long will you whet
Others' swords on your stone,
Continuing yet
Not to cut with your own?

trans: A. J. Arberry

THE ORANGES
by Abu Dharr (d. 1208)

The serried hosts stood man to man,
Determined either side to win,
Here Turk, there Ethiopian,
Their battle-field an orange-skin!

And when the armies began to fight
I never saw a sight so sweet;
The duskies put the blonds to flight,
For they had never known defeat.

But then the pale-faced Turks again
Took heart, and rallied to the fray;
They battled back with might and main,
They fought like heroes all the day.

It is the common rule of war
To fill with tears the watchers' eyes;
But this proved the exception, for
The watchers smiled in glad surprise.

trans: A. J. Arberry

BUBBLING WINE
by Abu Zakariya (d. 1249)

Spilled into the cup
The wine flames up,
Wreathing it entire
In robes of fire.

Now above the wine
Bright bubbles shine;
Greater wonder eye
May ne'er espy.
See, the wine's aflame;
Yet o'er the same
Dancing hailstones spin,
The wine's own kin.

trans: A. J. Arberry

Ethiopia

THE POTTER
(oral traditional)

Down there a poor woman
Pottery   she molds
Through night and day she fasted
Who   Taught   her   The knowledge
Out of clay   she makes pottery
And man from dust was created

* * * *

Mother   my beloved   You have gone
You created me in birth
To conceive you within me
Now   is my turn to ask you
Remain moving in my stomach
In the day of starvation
I might need to feed on you.

* * * *

To sleep with husband
In comfort   I delighted
With him on leather beds
I looked around
The dead
Were scattered on the ground

* * * *

In sickness you witnessed me
"Intoxicated" you shouted
Why 'tej'   I have not tasted
Along journey   I come
For 'Injera' alone
I stumbled like a drunkard.

NOTE: Tej—an alcoholic drink
   Injera—Ethiopian bread
   Leather beds—wealth and richness

trans: Halim El-Dabh

TROUSERS OF WIND

(An oral traditional household song about a worthless
lover, sung by women as they work.)

Trousers of wind and buttons of hail;
A lump of Shoa earth, at Gondar nothing left;
A hyena bearing meat, led by a leather thong;
Some water in a glass left standing by the fire;
A measure of water thrown on the hearth;
A horse of mist and a swollen ford;
Useless for anything, useful to no one;
Why am I in love with such a man as he?

trans: Sylvia Pankhurst

Zanzibar

SONG OF THE POOR MAN
(Anonymous, modern)

Give me a chair
and let me sit in your midst
and praise poverty
and want.

The face of a poor man
stays all crumped up
by reason of the hunger and thirst
which are in his stomach.

A poor man knows not
how to eat with a rich man.
When he starts eating fish
he eats its head.

Go and invite him
who has no bread
to come and eat crumbs
and thorns in the platters.

A poor man is nobody
because he has nothing.
Though nobly born
he is granted no favour.

A poor man is a snake—
his brothers avoid him

because of the misery
of the poverty-stricken.

But when a poor man is ill,
it leads his people
to show him kindness;
when a rich man is ill,
to light a lamp
he must wait for a slave.

trans: Anselm Hollo

Egypt

SALAH JAHIN is a young Egyptian who is essentially a satirist and cartoonist for the Cairo weekly *Sabah al-Khayr*. He is especially known for his cartoons which are critical of Egyptian society. His serious drawings appear in a volume of his poetry entitled *Rubaiyat*.

QUATRAINS

A marble mausoleum solemnly holds the rich
A hole without a bier holds a wretched one
I strolled by them . . . and wondered
From them both rose the same stench
Wonder!

From the fang of Time, my soul, there is no escape
One day will come you'll need some faith
My soul quivered and echoed "Faith in what?"
"Faith in what?" I've been asking for a long time
Wonder!

Beyond the window, clouds rain and thunder
It doesn't bother me—said I—it makes no difference
I changed my mind an hour later
I was in the street . . . a hole in my shoe
Wonder!

My heart got stuck in a long necked bottle
I had one drink and two and five and ten
I met men wine turns into wild beasts

I met men wine turns into pure beings
Wonder!

If there was peace on earth and calm and safety,
If there were no poor cowards and fear
If man was master of his destiny
I'd give the world a thousand sons
Wonder!

Spring came bouncing and found me sad
Spring called and found me silent
He laid some flowers by my side and left
What use are flowers to the dead
Wonder!

Winter stormed in and closed the doors
Spared the sun rays thin as cobwebs
Many things die during the winter night
But many more refuse to die
Wonder!

trans: Samir M. Zoghby

Sudan

MUHAMMAD AL-FĪTŪRI is a young man born of an Egyptian mother and a Sudanese father in the Bah al-ghazal region of the Sudan. He has published two volumes of verse and is building a reputation as a fine poet. He lives in Alexandria, Egypt.

THE KNELL

the fire of our victims
flows in our sinews
let us lean awhile on the bones of our dead
and awhile let us be silent

* * * *

the belfry of an old church, a perturbed monk
a cloud scratching its thighs passes over the horizon
a man without a neck
a woman slipping on the pavement
a cat gasping at the bottom of the steps
the lament of a tolling knell
draws a half circle in the heavenly vault
and tolls

* * * *

old birds
mummies, evidence of graves
pull their brown hair over the bridges
burn incense

and crush Father Time
whose crowd is that?
i followed it, fell dead, and was overcome by weakness
for whom then?
o world of sinners and fools
the fire has swept over the earth
for whom?

* * * *

o shame
hypocrisy is still the king of shades
and poets
prophets
and strangers
have unsheeted laughter
out of tears
and weave the dream of a griffin
while thrones and idols
are swept away by the broom of Father Time
old caesar
idol of idols
the Sultan servant of Islam
closed down the hatch of his vault
and slept.

trans: Samir Zoghby

I AM A NEGRO

Say it and cry aloud
Say it without shame
Without cowardness   Confront
The faces of human crowds
I am a Negro
Of Negro ancestry is my father
And Negro is my mother

I am black
Black with liberty
I possess the ownership of freedom
My land   Africa
Long live   my land
Long live   Africa

* * * *

My land the whites have molested
Abused by the oppressor's occupation
Let my life become a sacrificial offering
And like me my children shall be martyrs
Behind death behind the land
Echoes the cry of my forefathers
My descendants
You are severed from your heritage
Until the winds
Have swept the persecutor's ashes

* * * *

My children you are severed from your fathers
Until the agressor tumbles in disaster
Stripped from the shrouds of oppression
Until the land explodes with light
And in victory the black flag
Shines highest
Until history's forehead
Responds in the pride of joy

* * * *

The dawn pounds over
The walls of darkness
Listen to the song of victory
For here the oppressor
Claimed a failure

Falling in the abyss of terror
Here my people have risen from their trance
With naked chest
The black deluge
Chasing across the fortified rock
Witness
Here is Africa the great
Glittering
In the light of dawn.

trans: Halim El-Dabh

Somaliland

'ABDILLAAHI MUUSE, born toward the end of the last century, holds the title "The Keeper of the Quran" because he memorized the entire holy book. His poem *An Elder's Reproof to his Wife* is said to be autobiographical.

AN ELDER'S REPROOF TO HIS WIFE

A stream flowing steadily over a stone does not wet its core,
But on fertile soil water brings forth fresh grass,
Termite mounds when spoken to give no response,
A fool's mind is like a house barred,
When one tells people something, they profit by it,
But you, may God change you, are made worse by advice.
There is some remedy for the fools who listen to you,
But there is no medicine for a bad wife who refuses good
                                        advice;
And I was born with nobility of mind and am not readily
                                        disturbed by trifles.
My dissatisfaction goes back even to the times that I
                        visited you after our engagement.
Sometimes a fully laden vessel founders with great loss
                                        of property,
And certainly I received no return at all for the rifles
                        and camels I gave as bridewealth,
Again and again you wearied me, when the word "obey"
                        brought no response.
Neglect, beating, or divorce,
On one of these three I am resolved: make your choice!

                        trans: B. W. Andrzjewski and I. M. Lewis

FAARAH NUUR, who died about 1930, played an important part in emancipating his people from their bondage to a rival clan. He is of particular interest because he was one of the few Somalis of his time who were aware of the far-reaching significance of the first steps in the partitioning of his country by European powers.

THE LIMITS OF SUBMISSION

Over and over again to people
I show abundant kindness.

* * * *

If they are not satisfied
I spread out bedding for them
And invite them to sleep.

If they are still not satisfied,
The milk of the camel whose name is Suub
I milk three times for them,
And tell them to drink it up.

* * * *

If they are still not satisfied,
The homestead's ram,
And the fat he-goat I kill for them.

* * * *

If they are still not satisfied,
The plate from Aden
I fill with ghee for them.

* * * *

If they are still not satisfied,
A beautiful girl
And her bridal house I offer them.

* * * *

If they are still not satisfied,
I select livestock also
And add them to the tribute.

* * * *

If they are still not satisfied,
"Oh brother-in-law, oh Sultan, oh King!"
These salutations I lavish upon them.

* * * *

If they are still not satisfied,
At the time of early morning prayers I prepare
The dark grey horse with black tendons,
And with the words "Praise to the Prophet" I take
The iron-shafted spear,
And drive it through their ribs
So that their lungs spew out;
Then they are satisfied!

trans: B. W. Andrzjewski and I. M. Lewis

MODERN LOVE SONGS

I.
A flash of lightning does not satisfy thirst,
What then is it to me if you just pass by?

II.
It is the custom of the Somali,
To mock a man who has fallen in love.

III.
One does not hurry past a dying man,
Before I enter the grave, spare a word for me.

IV.
When you die you will enter the earth,
Let not the preacher then turn you from your love-song.

V.
Is it lightning far distant from me,
That I have strained for vainly?

VI.
The girl for whom I have withered like a stick,
Are you telling me to despair of ever attaining?

VII.
Until I die I shall not give up the love-song,
Oh God, forgive me my shortcomings.

VIII.
Oh, doctor, I have a pain in my heart,
Give me treatment, but don't put me in hospital!

NOTE: These verses are a modern love-song form broadcast
   on radio and widely heard even in the interior of Somaliland. The style was devised by a lorry driver some twenty
   years ago.

                              trans: B. W. Andrzejewski and I. M. Lewis

EUROPE

In classical times the black slave Aesop contrived fables for the instruction of his masters which still delight children in our time. Terence (Terentius Africanus) came to Rome from Africa as a slave to become the finest playwright of his age. Cultivated Romans admired his plays because of their exquisite style and their lofty moral tone. In fact Terence, the African, is generally held to be the inventor of the polite comedy. His influence is felt in the whole history of European theater and continues still in works of Molière, Shaw, and the comedies of manners.

The roll of black names in the history of Western literature would certainly be longer if it were not for the age-old European habit of hiding the black skeletons in family closets. For example, Antonio Vieira, the father of classical literary Portuguese, was discovered to be a Negro quite by chance. Vieira was a monk and an active political and social reformer. His enemies had him tried by the Inquisition as a heretical Jew, counting on his appearance to convict him. An array of witnesses came forward to swear that Vieira was not a Jew, but an African Negro. When he was set free, Vieira wrote a letter to the Vatican which damned the Holy Office in Portugal in such convincing terms that Pope Clement X forthwith suppressed it.

For many years after the brilliant rule of the Moors of
Spain had ended, a black skin still marked a man as a Moor
and therefore both chivalrous and cultivated. Thus it is
understandable how in the sixteenth century Juan Latino, a
black house slave of a noble Cordoban family, could rise to
become professor at the University of Granada and an inti-
mate of royalty. His ornate poetry was the example of artifi-
ciality and pretentiousness Cervantes chose to lampoon in
Don Quixote. Yet Juan Latino's poems actually bespeak a
passionate African nature. Hired to instruct the daughter of
a prominent family in Latin, he taught the conjugation of
amo amas amat so cogently that presently his young pupil,
Dona Ana, bore him a child. After their marriage, Juan
Latino gained such public esteem that he dared to write the
King of Spain:

If our black face, O King, seems to your ministers odious, 1.5
We Ethiops find your white ones no more to our taste.

Far more important in Europe's literary history than either
of these black Latins was Alexander Pushkin, the mulatto
poet and playwright who occupies the same place in Russian
literature as Shakespeare in that of England. Peter the Great
brought Pushkin's great-grandfather, Hannibal, to Russia in
order to prove that an African's capacities were no less than
those of a European. This black Ethiopian had a distinguished career in the Russian army and the court and married one of the great beauties of that day.

His descendant, Alexander Pushkin, was a lazy student,
who preferred to spend his time listening to the tales and
songs of his father's serfs than with his books. At the age of
fifteen, however, he composed a poem that changed the
whole course of Russian literature. It was the first great
writing in the Russian vernacular and it seized the imagination of the whole country. In its lines and in those of Push-

kin's subsequent works the Russians heard the sound of themselves for the first time. Pushkin wrote of love with a tenderness that established tradition of Russian romanticism. In a day of autocracy and tyranny he spoke out eloquently for liberty and justice, and his stinging wit constantly involved him in duels. In fact he became so inured to dueling that he once permitted an opponent to fire the first shot while he finished eating a handful of cherries.

A favorite of the Czar—sought after as the wittiest man of his day, idolized by the masses—Pushkin always thought of himself as a black man. He wrote:

An ever idle scapegrace, hideous descendant of Negroes, brought up in savage simplicity, I pleasure the young beauties with the unbridled furies of my African passion.

When Pushkin first heard Africa music it was "as if his flesh remembered some fabulous long ago. . . ." In his poetry, Pushkin adhered to a model that seems to be rootedly African. On the one hand, he used poetry like a sword—against his enemies and against injustice. On the other, Pushkin reached out through his poetry to embrace reality. "He is the echo of the world," said one critic, "an obedient and melodious echo that moves from realm to realm passionately responding to everyone. . . ." Another adds, "Pushkin listened eagerly to the call of the sky, the earth, the throbbing of the heart . . . A giant of the spirit, he embraces all, sees and hears everything."

The other great black figures in European literature were also warlike and Faustian in their appetites. General Alexander Dumas, the black Haitian general, so threatened to overshadow Napoleon in the wars of revolutionary France that Napoleon had him retired from military service. This giant black man was the greatest swordsman of his time. He could lift two men on one leg and hop around the room in a dance and once fought three duels in a single day. There can be little doubt that his son, the great novelist, modeled his hero, D'Artagnan, after his gallant father. But Alexander the novelist outstripped Alexander the general.

Alexander Dumas was the most prolific and best-paid writer who ever lived, publishing more than twelve hundred books and plays and many times that many articles for newspapers. His income from this literary torrent came to more than ten million dollars in the currency of the time, but this great mulatto novelist spent his fortune as fast as he earned it. His appetite for pleasure was as colossal as his literary sales, which, even in this day of mass distribution, seem prodigious. Between 1870 and 1884, 2,845,000 volumes and 80,000,000 subscription parts of his work were sold. Michlet, the critic: "A man? No, he is an element like an inextinguishable flame or a mighty river."

Dumas' greatest work turned out to be his illegitimate son, Alexander Dumas III, author of *Camille* and founder of the modern realistic theater. His cooly observant intelligence, translated in theatrical terms, turned the French theater away from bombast and artifice to serious thought. A member of the French Academy, he was also one of the wits of his age. Once a young artist made the mistake of teasing him about his ancestry. "Will you tell us, Monsieur Dumas, what was your great-grandfather?"

"He was an ape. My ancestry began where yours ends."

Spain

JUAN LATINO (Juan de Sessa), born in African Guinea about 1516 was brought to Spain at the age of twelve. After he graduated from the University at Granada, he became a professor of Rhetoric, Greek, and Latin. His life spanned the greatest period in Spain's history and he became a luminary of the Spanish Renaissance. When Don Juan of Austria (son of Emperor Charles V of Spain) won his celebrated victory over the Turks, Latino wrote *Austriad,* which is like a long African "praise song" for the victor of Lepanto. Latino died around 1606.

from AUSTRIAD

Autorem res magna petit, nascique poeta
Debuerat fratris, Summe Philippe tuo.
Unicus est victor, scriptorem quaerirat unum,
Res nova vult vatem Regibus esse novum
Auribus alme tuis non haet victoria Ponto est
Audita, hic scriptor nec fuit orbe satus
Aethiopum terris venit qui gesta Latinus
Austriadae mira carminis arte canat.

· · · · · · · · · · · ·

Princeps nunc fato regnis concessus avitis . . .
Principis ipsa tui mater, conjexque Philippi
Regina Hispanis vixeris alma diu.
Tu regem facias hunc pulchra prole parentem
Natorum natos Regina mater alas.

(A great event seeks an author; the poet for your brother,
great Philip, was due to be born. The victor is unique; he
seeks a unique bard. The new deed desires that the kings
have a new poet. This victory on the seas, benign one, was
heard by your ears. This writer was not engendered in this
region; he comes, Latino, from the land of the Ethiopians to
sing the marvelous deeds of Austria with the art of song.

.   .   .   .

Lo now a prince is granted by fate to the kingdom ancestral
. . . Mother is she of thy new-born prince, and wife of King
Philip; Hail to thee, fertile Queen, long may you now make
this king the father of glorious offspring. May there be sons
of your sons, nurtured, Queen Mother, from thee.)

Russia

ALEXANDER PUSHKIN (1799–1837), often called the father of
Russian literature, was descended from an old aristocratic family
on his father's side and on his mother's from an Ethiopian general
named Hannibal. He was proud of his African origins and he
wrote a short novel about his black ancestor entitled *The Negro
of Peter the Great.* Among the other works of Pushkin are
Eugene Onegin, Boris Godunov, and numerous volumes of
poetry.

WITH FREEDOM'S SEED

With freedom's seed the desert sowing,
I walked before the morning star;
From pure and guiltless fingers throwing—
Where slavish plows had left a scar—
The fecund seed, the procreator;
Oh, vain and sad disseminator,
I learned then what lost labors are . . .
Graze if you will, you peaceful nations,
Who never rouse at honor's horn!
Should flocks heed freedom's invocations?
Their part is to be slain or shorn,
Their dower the yoke their sires have worn
Through snug and sheeplike generations.

trans: Babette Deutsch

MESSAGE TO SIBERIA

Deep in the Siberian mine,
Keep your patience proud.
The bitter toil shall not be lost,
The rebel thought unbowed.

The sister of misfortune, hope,
In the under-darkness dumb,
Speaks joyful courage to your heart:
The day desired will come.

And love and friendship pour to you
Across the darkened doors,
Even as round your galley-beds
My free music pours.

The heavy-hanging chains will fall,
The walls will crumble at a word,
And Freedom greet you in the light,
And brothers give you back the sword.

trans: Max Eastman

France

AUGUSTE LACAUSSADE, born in 1817 on the Ile de la Réunion just off the African coast, was one of France's most gifted Negro poets. His most important works are *Les Salaziennes* and *Poemes et paysages*. He was honored by the French Academy, receiving the Prix Bordin in 1852, and in 1860 was elected to membership in the *Légion d'honneur*. Lacaussade died in France in 1897.

from LES SALAZIENNES

My lips from this day forgot how to smile.
At the age when one blesses, I began to curse
This country whose arrogance destroyed the pride
Of a heart made for glory and for liberty!
They circumscribed my road, they limited my career.
To my thirst for knowledge they forbade the spring
From which science and art flow in wide torrents,
They riveted my youth to an insulting repose.

ALEXANDRE DUMAS fils (1824–95), best known for his novel
and play *La Dame aux camélias,* had Haitian blood on his
father's side. One of his youthful love affairs, with the Countess
Nesselrode, inspired several verses and these appear with an
account of a meeting between Madame, father, and son in Dumas
père's *Causeries* ("Chats").

verses to THE LADY OF THE PEARLS

We set out yesterday upon a winter drive,
Pressed each to each to keep the cold away,
And through a darkening world did strive
To bear love's deathless spring upon the way.

. . . .

And when the time of flowers is come, I'll walk apart
To muse upon the name carved in that stone,
The sweet name which imprisons all my heart,
Effaced, perhaps, by winds that round it have made moan.

Dear sharer of that day, ah! where will you be then?
I, perhaps, uncompanioned, hearing not your feet;
Will you be treading happy ways again?
And I be left, Winter in Summer's heat?

For Winter's not the roads we looked upon,
Now empty; not the angry blast and frore:
It is the sunless heart, the spirit dark and dun;
It is what I shall be when you are there no more.

trans: Gerard Hopkins

RENÉ MARAN, born at Fort-de-France in Martinique in 1887, is known to English-speaking readers for his novel *Batouala*. In 1942 he received the Grand Prix Broguette-Gonin from the French Academy. He has published a volume of verse as well as numerous novels that contain poems and songs based on African folklore. This poem is like a blues.

HUMAN SOUL

I am one of those troubled hearts,
Fearing the night, fearing the day.
I know not if I have a hate,
I do know that I had a love.

If only I were understood
By those who do not understand!
But what can I do? I'm in love,
And my heart gets so out of hand!

What good is it for you to say
Those kind words that just lure me on?
Would that I could always be gay!
But always I am woe-begone.

I think that I envy no man;
I've never been an infidel.
But I've suffered since life began,
From loving without being loved.

And now that I find I'm adored
By someone who holds me embraced,
I don't know if I'm still enamoured
Or if all my love's been effaced.

trans: Mercer Cook

CREOLES

Whereas North America was settled by families, the French, Spanish, and Portuguese colonies to the South were at first largely military missions, staffed by men. These Latin-American colons took mistresses and sometimes wives among the Indians and blacks they ruled. They fathered children of mixed blood and, together with their offspring, were contemptuously referred to as "criollas" or "creoles" by those who stayed safely at home in Europe. The term Creole which at first meant emigré—mixed blood—bastard—rich upstart— or all four—, became a proud title when the colonies grew rich and the rising Creole families outstripped the stay-at-homes who had scorned them. Thus in Louisiana, where both blacks and whites owned slaves, it was perfectly logical to speak of *white creoles* and *black creoles* and to take pride or shame in either title.

In legalistic North America one drop of Negro blood has been enough to put a man beyond the pale, but Latin Americans could not choose to be so finicky, especially after the revolutions against Spanish rule. Many of the leaders and heroes in those wars were men of mixed blood, both Indian and African—Ribadavia, first president of Argentina; Guerrero, who liberated Mexico from Spain and abolished slavery there; Maceo and Marti, twin champions of freedom in Cuba; the mighty trio of Haiti—pale Toussaint, gigantic black Christophe, ruthless Dessalines; and gossip holds that even Simon Bolivar, the neurotic, beak-nosed George Washington of the southern continent was a *zambo* (mixed blood) and first swore to free his native land at the Hill of the Slaves in Rome. It is true, at any rate, that Bolivar, like many Latin patriots, rode with black generals at his side and led black troops who had a double thirst for freedom—from Spain and from their masters.

As the children of white colonialists, as fellow revolutionaries and full Catholics, the octoroons and the mulattos of Latin America could not be kept out, as were their brothers in the self-righteous North. Instead they were assimilated. They rose in the world and often chose to forget their background in the pleasure of living and writing like a Spaniard, Portuguese, or Frenchman. Many of the greatest and most venerated figures in Latin-American literature—de Assis in Brazil, Dario in Nicaragua—were known to have black blood, but it became both unpleasant and inconvenient to mention this. As Guillén writes:

> *Yesterday they called me "nigger"*
> *so I should get mad;*
> *but he who called thus*
> *was as black as I am.*
> *You pretend to be so white—*
> *but I know your grandmother.*

The Latin-American upper classes therefore took in and took credit for all the mulatto and mestizo writers, by honoring them as national literary ornaments or by linking them to some European school. Meanwhile, the masses of blacks and Indians, left behind in the poor barrios, could be thought of as brutish lower orders without any cultivation. This is

why the cultural and political achievements of blacks in
South America are as little known to us as were those of
North American blacks. In the North the caste line kept
blacks out. In the South the class system swallowed them up
and they disappeared.

The first American to speak out eloquently against racial
injustice was Vieira, the half-African Portuguese monk, who
after reforming the fiscal system of the Kingdom of Portugal
sailed over to Brazil to spend the rest of his life attacking
the cruelties of black and Indian slavery. Vieira's orations
against slavery are regarded as the best models of classical
literary Portuguese. In an Easter Sunday sermon, preached
before the viceroy, his ministers and the leading slave owners of Brazil, Vieira thundered:

*Your mansions, your opulence, your fine robes and mantles drip
with the blood of your unhappy slaves . . . There is no other
country in the world where the devil could obtain a better bar-
gain than amongst you. He has no need to offer you mansions,
cities or even hamlets. He has only to show you one or two slaves
to have you fall in adoration at his feet. "For a Negro your soul!
This Negro will be your slave for life, but in return your soul
will be my slave in all eternity" . . .*

The dignitaries went back to their money-grubbing and to
their black mistresses, but with an uneasy conscience. Ac-
cordingly it has not been such a shameful or painful thing
to be black in Brazil. There African languages and customs
stayed alive. Indeed, nowhere in the Latin world was African
drumming outlawed so consistently suppressed as in the British colonies. Thus the sinuous, complex dance and movement
style of Africa could survive intact in the Caribbean world
and flower in a host of dance forms which became the basis
for national culture and the common property of mankind.
Name the rumba, the conga, the samba, the tango, the

mambo, the fox trot and you speak a black *creole,* and, at the same time, an international language.

New modes of speech developed alongside the new dance forms of Latin America and the Caribbean. The varied creole dialects of Brazil, Cuba, the Guineas, and the French and British West Indies at first were viewed by scholars as so many childish imitations of European languages. Further research has shown them all to be branches of a newly emerging language, *creole,* which is a West African linguistic adjustment to European contact.

When creole speakers turned their hand to letters, they brought to their work the resources of this newly minted language and its store of fresh emotional nuances. So in Brazil, de Assis wrote stories and novels hailed as the equal of anything in the Iberian tradition. In Nicaragua, Dario, the mestizo man of color, introduced a new tone to Spanish poetry and became the literary leader of his age in Paris and elsewhere. One by one, in every country where blacks dwelt, they produced a creole poetry, part-European, but delicately reflecting the moods of exotic tropical cultures. The Louisiana of rich black slave owners fostered its own high-toned literateurs who published in Paris. Every Caribbean land produced first rate poets. Turn to the poems of Derek Walcott of St. Lucia. Robert Graves says Walcott "handles English with a closer understanding of its inner magic than most (if not any) of his English-born contemporaries." Walcott brings a Shakespearean skill in English to the evocation of his Windward Islands. The poetry of Darío undoubtably rings as true in Spanish.

In Haiti a school of vernacular poets grew up, under the influence of the Harlem revival, beginning with the work of Roumer and continued by Marcellin, Brouard, and Jacques Roumain, who showed his greatness in the novel *Masters of the Dew* and was beaten to death in a Haitian jail because he spoke out against injustice. These radical Haitians utilized their native folklore and saw themselves as Africans in the New World. In Cuba, under the influence of the ethnologist, Ortiz, poets emerged who incorporated the sound and rhythm of Afro-Cuban dances in their verse. Then Nicholas Guillén broke through to a truly Negro art, structuring his poems around black rhythms and building them on patterns of sound meant to be recited to drum accompaniment. At the same time Guillén masterfully employed the passionate imagry and the startling shifts of direction so characteristic of African art.

Yet the giant of the Afro-American tradition is unquestionably Aimé Césaire. Coming to Paris from Martinique in the 30's, stimulated by the black renaissance of Harlem, Césaire conspired with Senghor and Damas to create an art based in the aesthetics of Africa. Senghor remarked about his friend that "he used his pen like Louis Armstrong his trumpet or the devotees of voodoo their tom-toms." His book-length manifesto—*On a Return to My Native Land*—brought new flexibility to the language of poetry, but it was a black flexibility, dealing in constant and dramatic shifts of emotion —from anger to affirmation, from tenderness to ferocity. In Césaire the black world acquired a great poet who immediately moved beyond and ahead of cool and careful European masters like Yeats, Pound, Eliot, and Graves. Césaire's poetry has the lyricism of Dylan, but is a call to arms. (A.L.)

Brazil

ANTÔNIO GONÇALVES DIAS (1823–64), Brazil's first great poet, was part white, Indian, and Negro. Prior to 1900, he was the only specifically American poet to be recognized in Central Europe. He was also a distinguished ethnologist who devoted many years to the study of Indian languages.

from SONG OF EXILE

There are palm trees in my homeland
Where a "sabia" is singing,
But the birds who warble here
Do not sing as in my country.

There are more stars in our heavens,
And more flowers in our meadows;
In our forests is more life,
And our life has more affection . . .

God grant that I may not die here
In this place, without returning,
And without enjoying pleasures
Which I find not in this country,
And the palm trees I would see
Where the "sabia" is singing.

trans: Frances Ellen Buckland

LUIS GONZAGA PINTO DA GAMA (1830–82), born in San Salvador, Brazil, of a black Brazilian woman and a Portuguese nobleman, was sold into slavery at the age of ten. Eventually, he ran off and became variously soldier, policeman, civil clerk, and poet. His famous "comic ballads" were published under the pseudonym Getulino in the satiric periodical *The Lame Devil* and in an abolitionist newspaper. In the first Republican Congress of Sâo Paulo, he called for the immediate abolition of all slaves. He declared before the court: "Every slave who kills his master, whatever the circumstances, does so in legitimate self-defense."

WHO I AM

Am I a black man or a goat?
What does it matter?
There are billygoats in every caste.
The species is vast:
There are grey ones and striped ones
Mulattos, pampa dwellers and country dwellers
Black goats, white goats;
Let's be frank:
There are plebians and nobles,
Rich billygoats, poor billygoats
Wise, important billies
And merchants, too . . .
Here on this good earth
Everything amazes and enrages.
Nobles, counts and duchesses,
Rich dames and marchionesses,
Deputies, Senators,
Gentlemen, administrators
Lovely ladies of quality,
Of haughty mein,
Inflated little princes,
Proud little noblemen,

Monks, bishops, cardinals:
All the imperial fanfare,
The poor, the rich—
Everyone wears my horns:
In the brave militia
Great billygoats
Guards, chiefs, sargeants,
Brigadiers, colonels,
Intrepid marshals,
Brilliant generals,
Captains of war and sea;
Everything amazes and enrages.
In the supreme Eternity,
Home of the Divinity
Billy goats are sanctified—
Adorned (by us);
In the chorus of little angels
Bleat many little goats;
Syringa's lover has wooly hair and smells;
The god Mendes, they say, has horns;
Baby Jupiter sucked goats milk;
And according to ancient myth
The faun, too, was a goat;
In Pluto's dominion
A billy studies the Koran;
In clean and beautiful places
Goathood is sung in praises;
So, since everyone has a tail,
Why all the fuss?
Let there be peace and gaiety!
Let us all screw and play!
Cease this warfare—
We are all members of the goatherd

                         trans: Anna Lomax

JOAQUIM MARIA MACHADO DE ASSIS (1839–1908), one of Brazil's most famous writers, has been called by one of his countrymen, José Verissimo, "the highest expression of our literary genius; the most eminent figure of our literature." Although very little of his poetry has been translated into English, his novels *Epitaph for a Small Winner* and *Dom Casmurro* gained high critical acclaim in translation.

BLUE FLY

It was a blue fly with wings of pomegranate gold,
    Daughter of Cathay or Hindustan,
Springing from a deep flesh-colored rose among the leaves,
    On a certain night in summer time.
And she buzzed and flew about, and flew about and buzzed,
    Shining in the splendor of the sun
And the brightness of the moon. She shone much brighter
                              than
    Diamonds of the Great Mogul would shine . . .

Then the man, extending forth his callous coarsened hand,
    Only used to carpenters' rough work,
With a gesture laid a hold of that resplendent fly,
    Curious to re-examine her . . .

He examined her to such a point, in such a way,
    Torn and tarnished, nauseated, vile,
She succumbed. And thus that subtle and fantastic thing,
    Thus that vision vanished from the man.

Now today when he goes by, with cardamom and
    Aloe on his head, and stylish airs,
It is said he has gone crazy, that he does not know
    How it was he lost his bright blue fly.

trans: Frances Ellen Buckland

MARIO DE ANDRADE (1839–1945), born in São Paulo, Brazil, was a perfect example of the ethnic trinity of his country: Indian, Negro, and Portuguese. He has been called the "Pope of Futurism," a writer who in every volume attempted a new and radical mode of expression. He was active in an attempt to introduce a national language into several Latin-American nations. This activity reached its height in his *Macunaima*. His complete works fill nineteen volumes.

ASPIRATION

The sweetness of poverty like this . . .
To lose everything yours, even the egoism of being,
So poor that you can only belong to the crowd . . .
I gave away everything mine, I spent all my being,
And I possess only what in me is common to all . . .
The sweetness of poverty like this . . .

I am not lonely any more, I am dissolved among equal men!

I have walked. Along my way
The emphatic mark of my steps
Remained on ground wet with morning dew.
Then the Sun ascended, heat vibrated in the air
In golden particles of light and warm breath.

The ground burned and hardened.
The mark of my feet is now invisible . . .
But the Earth remains, the tenderly dumb Earth,
And growing, grieving, dying in Earth,
The always equal men remain . . .

And I feel larger, equalizing myself to the equal men! . . .

                                                    trans: John Nist

RONDEAU FOR YOU
to Conto de Barros (1924)

From you, Rose, I do not like
To accept only this slow hug
That you give me
Or only this moist kiss
That you give me ...
I do not for a single reason:
From everything you tell me
I see that in your breast
Sobs the well-made heart of you.
And then I imagine
That together with the slender body
The dark little body
That you give me
Together with your loveliness
The maddening charm and laughter
That you give me
It would be something if I too owned
What hides behind your face, Rose:
The thought, the soul, the grief of you.

trans: John Nist

JORGE DE LIMA, born in 1893 at Uniao, Alagoas, Brazil, is a
mulatto who celebrated the Negro as few Brazilian poets have
done. He has been called a "restless creative genius who possesses
a temperament that is constantly renewing itself." Among his
many collections of verse is *Poemas Negros* (1946).

THE WORDS WILL RESURRECT

The words have grown old inside men
And separated into islands,

The words have mummified in the mouths of legislators;
The words have rotted in the promises of tyrants;
The words mean nothing in the speeches of politicians.
And the Word of God is one despite the sacrilege
                              of the men of Babel,
Despite the sacrilege of the men of today.
And can it be that the immortal word will sicken?
And can it be that the great Semitic word will disappear?
And can it be that the poet was not designated to give
                              the word new life?
To pick it from the surface of the waters and offer it
                    again to the men of the continent?
And was he not appointed to restore its essence,
                    and to reconstitute its magic content?
Does the poet not see the communion of languages,
When men will reconquer the attributes lost with The Fall,
And when the nations founded after Babel will be destroyed?
When all the confusion is undone,
Will the poet not speak from wherever he is,
To all the men on earth, in one single language—
                    the language of the Spirit?
But should you live sunk in time and in space,
You will not understand me, brother!

trans: John Nist

PAPA JOHN

Papa John withered like a rootless stick.——
        Papa John is going to die.
Papa John rowed the boats.——
            He dug the earth.
            He made spring from the ground
            The emerald of leaves—coffee, cane, cotton.
Papa John dug up more emeralds
        Than pioneer Paes Leme.

Papa John's daughter had the breasts of a cow
        For his master's children to suck:
        When her breasts dried up, Papa John's daughter
        Also withered while fastened to
        A pressing iron.
        Papa John's skin stuck to the tips
        Of whips.
        Papa John's strength stayed on the handle
        Of hoe and of scythe.
        Papa John's wife the white
        Man stole and made her a nurse.
Papa John's blood dissolved in the good blood
        Like a lump of crude sugar
        In a pan of milk.——
        Papa John was a horse for his master's children to
                                                        mount
        Papa John could tell such beautiful stories
        That you felt like crying.
        Papa John is going to die.
        The night outside is as black as Papa John's skin.
        Not one star in the sky.
        It looks like the witchcraft of Papa John.

                        trans: John Nist

Nicaragua

RUBÉN DARÍO (1867–1916), with his fusion of Spanish-Indian-Negro blood, led a movement which revitalized Spanish literature. He was king of the Parnassian school of poetry, surpassed by no one of his period in brilliance or in refinement. His complete poetic works are available in three different editions and a fine selection has been translated into English, entitled *Selected Poems* (1965).

TO COLUMBUS

Unfortunate admiral! Your poor America,
your beautiful, hot-blooded, virgin Indian love,
the pearl of your dreams, is now hysterical,
her nerves convulsing and her forehead pale.

A most disastrous spirit rules your land:
where once the tribesmen raised their clubs together,
now there is endless warfare between brothers,
the selfsame races wound and destroy each other.

The stone idol is gone, and in its place
a living idol sits upon a throne,
while every day the pallid dawn reveals
the blood and ashes in the fields of neighbors.

Disdaining kings, we give ourselves our laws
to the sound of cannons and of bugle-calls,
and now, on the sinister behalf of black kings,
each Judas is a friend of every Cain.

We love to drink the festive wines of France;
day after day we sing the *Marseillaise*
in our indigenous, semi-Spanish voices,
but end by roaring out the *Carmagnole*.

The treacheries of ambition never cease,
the dream of freedom lies in broken bits.
This crime was never committed by our chiefs,
by those to whom the mountains gave their arrows.

They were majestic, loyal, and great-hearted;
their heads were decorated with rare feathers.
Oh if the white men who came had only been
like the Aatahualpas and the Moctezumas!

When once the seed of the iron race from Spain
was planted in the womb of the Americas,
the heroic strength of great Castile was mixed
with the strength of our own Indians of the mountains.

Would to God that these waters, once untouched,
had never mirrored the white of Spanish sails,
and that the astonished stars had never seen
those caravels arriving at our shores!

The mountains saw how the natives, who were free
as eagles, came and went in the wild forest,
hunting the deer, the puma, and the bison
with the sure arrows they carried in their quivers.

A chief, though rough and bizarre, is worth far more
than a soldier who roots his glory in the mud,
who has caused the brave to groan beneath his car
or the frozen mummies of Incan lords to tremble.

The cross you brought to us is now decayed,
and after the revolution of the rabble,
the rabble writing today defiles the language
written by great Cervantes and Calderon.

A gaunt and feeble Christ walks through the streets,
Barabbas can boast of slaves and epaulets,
and the lands of Chibcha, Cuzco, and Palenque
have seen wild beasts acclaimed and decorated.

Evil mischance has placed afflictions, horrors,
wars, and unending fevers in our way:
Oh Christopher Columbus, unfortunate admiral,
pray to God for the world that you discovered!

trans: Lysander Kemp

ALLELUYA

Roses, rose-red and white, and green
boughs and bright corollas and fresh
bouquets. Happiness!

Nests in the warm trees,
eggs in the warm nests,
devotion. Happiness!

The kiss of this blonde girl,
and of this tawny girl,
and of this black girl. Happiness!

And the smooth belly of the girl
who is only fifteen and the harmony
of her arms. Happiness!

And the breath of the virgin forest,
of the virgin women,
and the sweet rhymes of daybreak.
Happiness! Happiness! Happiness!

trans: Lysander Kemp

Haiti

ISAAC TOUSSAINT L'OUVERTURE (1782–1854), born at En-
nery in Haiti, was the son of the Haitian liberator and governor
of Santo Domingo. He was one of those unusual individuals who
combine the qualities of charm, bravery, good looks, and physical
prowess with the ability to write well. His unpublished memoirs
are in Bordeaux, France, where he died.

FAREWELL

Shores of my native land
    What tears I have shed for you
When the winds with cruel command
    Called the hour of my adieu!
Borne by the ship, swift, light,
    Far from love, from the joys I knew,
The little thatched-roof vanished from sight
Of the one love my heart knew.

Strange the stars, all this other world,
    Strange the cities, the people I view,
This longing which my soul suffers
    'Mid sailors where fires blew,
And the sea—this supreme barrier,
    All tell my grief again too—
How far, how far the little thatched-roof
Of the one love my heart knew!

I have braved both storm and war,
    Strange lands with their stranger ways!

But nothing has dimmed your face for me
    Whether safe in port or at sea's mercy,
I kept on saying of you:
When shall I see the little thatched-roof
Of the one love my soul knew!

trans: Edna Worthley Underwood

EMILE ROUMER, born in 1903 in Jérémie, Haiti, was one of the founders of the important Haitian poetry journal *La Revue Indigène.* After a period of studies in France and England, he returned home to practice law. His published works include *Poèmes d'Haiti et de France* (1925) and *Nouveaux Poèmes* (1945).

THE PEASANT DECLARES HIS LOVE

HIGH-YELLOW of my heart, with breasts like tangerines,
you taste better to me than eggplant stuffed with crab,
you are the tripe in my pepper-pot,
the dumpling of my peas, my tea of aromatic herbs.
You are the corned beef whose customhouse is my heart,
my mush with syrup that trickles down the throat.
You are a steaming dish, mushroom cooked with rice,
crisp potato fries, and little fish fried brown . . .
My hankering for love follows you wherever you go.
Your bum is a gorgeous basket brimming with fruits and
                                                    meat.

A BLACK GIRL GOES BY

"Night-dark girl of the swaying hips."
LANGSTON HUGHES

Your walk sacerdotal and slow, undulant,
    So weary sometimes, with such air nonchalant,

Your grace, my memory long, long, will haunt.
Your loins both supple and fine that sway
Fling to my mind the black panther's way
To leap, to rage, at touch of javelin-tips.
My soul is cradled in moired silk crepe
To the sensual song of a woman's hips.

trans: Edna Worthley Underwood

OSWALD DURAND (1840–1906), born at Cap Haitien, Haiti,
was one of the best-loved poets of his land. An ardent nationalist,
he was also active in the government where he held several important offices. His famous poem *Choucoune* was popularized in
a song.

THE BLACK MAN'S SON

Like Lise, moreover, my mother was white,
Her eyes were blue where sleeping tears gleamed,
Whenever she blushed or in fear or delight,
Pomegranates burst into bloom it seemed.

Her hair was gold too! In wind and the light
It covered her forehead where pale griefs dreamed.
My father was blacker than I. Yet deemed
Sacred their union the Church and right.

Behold, strange contrast, on her white breast
A child as golden and brown as the maize,
Ardent, too, as the sun in our land always.
I, orphan, loved Lise at youth's intensest,
But her face grew pale at such words from me,
The Black Man's son held a terror, you see.

trans: Edna Worthley Underwood

JACQUES ROUMAIN (1907–44), born in Port-au-Prince, Haiti, became widely known internationally as a result of his political imprisonment and exile and subsequent return to his native land and a post in the foreign service of the government. He was one of the founders of the influential *Revue Indigène*. His novel *Gouverneurs de la Rosée* (1944) achieved world success and appeared in the United States in a translation by Langston Hughes under the title *Masters of the Dew* (1947). His poetry has been widely anthologized in many languages.

GUINEA

It's the long road to Guinea
Death takes you down
Here are the boughs, the trees, the forest
Listen to the sound of the wind in its long hair
                                of eternal night

It's the long road to Guinea
Where your fathers await you without impatience
Along the way, they talk
They wait
This is the hour when the streams rattle
                                like beads of bone

It's the long road to Guinea
No bright welcome will be made for you
In the dark land of dark men:
Under a smoky sky pierced by the cry of birds
Around the eye of the river
                    the eyelashes of the trees open on decaying light
There, there awaits you beside the water a quiet village,
And the hut of your fathers, and the hard ancestral stone
                                where your head will rest at last.

trans: Langston Hughes

JEAN BRIERRE, born in Haiti in 1909, first came to the attention of the English-speaking world when Edna Worthley Underwood included him in *The Poets of Haiti* (1782–1934). He
now lives in exile in Senegal and is still writing poetry.

HARLEM

I have seen you suffer in the midst of winters,
and your shadow erect amidst the street lamps
has told me often of its hunger at the doors
                                        of the eating houses.
I have seen you bleed at times on the sidewalks,
and I have not heard your agony make complaint.
I have seen you adorned in the springtime,
        bedecked in laughter and joy,
        dressed in sunshine and silk,
        singing and dancing,
        singing strange songs,
the heavy songs of sirens,
        of voyaging,
        of calls and of silence on forgotten seas,
        of bitter songs,
        ending with outbursts of laughter
        like mighty cymbals.
        I have seen you dancing in whirlwinds
        like the frenzied,
        celebrating some god hidden in the
        depths of you.
Where, O Harlem, do you sleep?
Perhaps you pluck the leaves of the last star
in your fragile cup
and find again at the portals of the dawn
        the trouble,
        the toil,
        the weariness,

the poverty,
the hour which sounds like a knell
and your heart, weary and alone
on the road, hostile and black.

trans: John F. Matheus

ROUSSAN CAMILLE (1915–61), born in Jacmel, Haiti, was active in poetry and in government affairs. He was the first secretary of the Haitian Legation in Paris, vice-consul in his country's New York Consulate, and once held a post in the Department of National Education. He was once editor-in-chief of the *Haiti Journal* and published a book of verse entitled *Assaut à la Nuit* (1940).

NOCTURNE

Wildness of haggard flights
through the jungle,
nurturer of revolts,
foster-father of despair and sin,
snare of the soul and the flesh,
night has never left me alone.

I embraced it so strongly,
so hated,
and so loved it,
that I carry it
in my black skin,
in my black eyes,
in my black heart.

I have eaten the purple fruit
of twilight gardens.
My very anguish has followed
the terrifying labyrinths of Midnight.

I have lent my ear
to dawn's muffled fanfares.
And I bring back
with the black ashes
of exhausted minutes
all the mystery unknown
to loveless eyes,
all the passionate memory
of warriors and amazons
who died long ago
of frightful wounds
somewhere in me
and in the night,
all the untouched freshness
of unknown streams,
and the strains of sorrowful multitudes.
When,
jostling the hours and the images,
my steps touch
the furthest limits of adventure
and of darkness,
if I hate the artificial song
of hypocritical lips,
it is because I share
in all the sufferings
and with all these worlds prostrated before the
        night's black prairies.

trans: Seth L. Wolitz

Louisiana

ARMAND LANUSSE (1812–67), born in New Orleans, Louisiana, was a leader in a political-literary society known as the free men of color. He held the position of principal of the Catholic School for Indigent Orphans of Color. In 1845 he compiled an important anthology of creole poetry entitled *Les Cenelles.*

EPIGRAM

"Do you not wish to renounce the Devil?"
Asked a good priest of a woman of evil
Who had so many sins that every year
They cost her endless remorse and fear.
"I wish to renounce him forever," she said,
"But that I may lose every urge to be bad,
Before pure grace takes me in hand,
Shouldn't I show my daughter how to get a man?"

trans: Langston Hughes

PIERRE DALCOUR (1800's), was a free colored of Louisiana who decided to spend most of his time abroad. His poetry appears in the anthology *Les Cenelles* edited by Armand Lanusse.

VERSE WRITTEN IN THE ALBUM OF MADEMOISELLE——

The evening star that in the vaulted skies
Sweetly sparkles, gently flashes,
To me is less lovely than a glance of your eyes
    Beneath their brown lashes.

trans: Langston Hughes

Cuba

JUAN FRANSICO MANZANO (1797–1854), born in Havana, was a slave who won his freedom through poetry. His sadistic mistress tortured him brutally for the "unnatural crime" of composing and reciting poetry. When he managed to escape, a group of Cuban writers purchased his freedom and he devoted himself to writing poetry. Among his published works are *Cantos a Lesbia* (1821), *Flores pasageras* (1830), *Zafiira* (1842), and *Autobiografia, cartas y versos* (1937).

MY THIRTY YEARS

When on my time of living I reflect,
Right from my cradle to the present date,
Only with trembling can I greet my fate,
Governed much more by terror than respect.

I wonder at the light I still have got,
Redeeming the dark suffering and shame
Of this my life, if it deserves that name,
The long endurance of a hopeless lot.

For thirty years I've known this world of pain,
For thirty years I've groaned beneath the war
Of cruel opression, lusting to pursue me.

But all the torment I've endured in vain
Is nothing to what one day is in store,
For her—oh, God!—who brought this torment to me.

trans: Oliver Cobarn & Ursula Lehrburger

PLACIDO (1809–44), born Gabriel de la Concepción Valdes in Havana, is one of Cuba's national heroes. He was the illegitimate son of a Spanish dancer and an Afro-Cuban. He wrote "Arcadian," bucolic and patriotic lyrics and, at the age of thirty-five, he was executed by the Spanish rulers of the island and became a martyr in Cuba's struggle for liberty. His *Poesias completas* were published in Paris in 1856.

FAREWELL TO MY MOTHER

(Written in the Chapel
of the Hospital de Santa Cristina
on the night before his execution)

If the unfortunate fate engulfing me,
The ending of my history of grief,
The closing of my span of years so brief,
Mother, should wake a single pang in thee,

Weep not. No saddening thought to me devote;
I calmly go to a death that is glory-filled;
My lyre, before it is forever stilled,
Breathes out to thee its last and dying note.

A note scarce more than a burden-easing sigh
Tender and sacred, innocent, sincere—
Spontaneous and instinctive as the cry
I gave at birth—And now the hour is here—
O God, thy mantle of mercy o'er my sins!
Mother, farewell! The pilgrimage begins.

trans: James Weldon Johnson

PRAYER TO GOD

O God of love unbounded! Lord supreme!
In overwhelming grief to Thee I fly.
Rending this veil of hateful calumny,

Oh let Thine arm of might my fame redeem!
Wipe Thou this foul disgrace from off my brow,
With which the world hath sought to stamp it now.

.   .   .   .

But if this lot Thy love ordains to me,
To yield to foes most cruel and unjust,
To die and leave my poor and senseless dust
The scoff and sport of their weak enmity,
Speak Thou, and then Thy purposes fulfill;
Lord of my life, work Thou Thy perfect will.

trans: Raoul Abdul

JOSÉ MARTÍ (1853–95), born in Havana, Cuba, did more than any other single person to secure Cuban independence. Trained in Spain as a lawyer, he returned to Cuba and was banished many times for his political activities. In an attempt to lead armed Cuban revolutionaries, he was killed in a skirmish with Spanish forces at Dos Rios. A gifted poet and prose writer, he was a precursor of the *modernista* movement. His writings are collected in seventy-three volumes as *Obras completas*.

SIMPLE VERSES

I am a sincere man
From where the palm tree grows,
And before I die I wish
To pour forth the verses from my soul.

.   .   .   .

I grow a white rose
In July as in January
For the sincere friend
Who gives me his frank hand.

And for the cruel one who tears out
The heart with which I live,
Neither thorn nor thistle do I grow;
I grow the white rose.

trans: Seymour Resnick

TWO COUNTRIES

Two countries have I: Cuba and the Night.
Or are the two one? Her majesty, the Sun
does not retreat well. With wide veils
and a carnation in her hand, silent Cuba
appears sad to me, like a widow.
I know what that bloodstained carnation is
that trembles in her hand.
My bosom is empty, it was destroyed
and there remains a void where the heart was.
Now is the hour to begin to die.
The Night is good for saying goodbye.
The light obstructs and the word humanizes.
The universe speaks better than man.
Which banner invites to battle the crimson flame.
I open the windows now. I stretch myself.
The change tears the petals of the carnation
like a cloud that disturbs the sky.
Cuba, the widow, passes.

trans: Mona Hinton

JOSÉ ZACARÍAS TALLET, born in 1893 in Cuba, is a poet and author of several dance compositions. His poetry is published in *Antologia de Poesia Negra Hispano-Americana* (edited by Emilio Ballagas) and *Black Orpheus.*

RUMBA

The climax of passion, the dancers are trembling
and ecstasy presses José to the ground.
The Bongo is thundering and in a mad whirl
the daemon has broken Tomasa's limbs.
Piqui-tiqui-pan, piqui-tiqui-pan!
Piqui-tiqui-pan, piqui-tiqui-pan!
The blackish Tomasa now falls to the ground
and down also falls Che Encarnación.
there they are rolling, convulsing, and twitching,
with whirling drum and raging Bongo
the rumba now fades with con-con-co-mabo!
And pa-ca, pa-ca, pa-ca, pa-ca!
Pam! pam! Pam!

trans: Sangodare Akanji

REGINO PEDROSO, born in 1896 in Cuba, is part Chinese and part Negro. As a youth he worked in the sugar, railroad, and steel industries as a day laborer. Later he was employed in the Ministry of Education and he was for many years a children's librarian. His published works include *Nosotros* (1933), *Antologia poética: 1918–1938,* (1939) and *Más allá canta el mar* (1939).

OPINIONS OF THE NEW STUDENT

Until yesterday I was polite and peaceful . . .

Last year I drank the yellow-leaved Yunnan tea
in fine cups of porcelain,

and deciphered the sacred texts of Lao-Tze,
of Mang-tze,
and of the wisest of the wise, Kung-fu-Tseu.

Deep in the shade of the pagodas
my life ran on, harmonious and serene,
white as the lilies in the pools,
gentle as a poem by Li Tai Po,
watching the loop-the-loop
of white storks at eve
against the screen of an alabaster sky.

But I have been awakened by the echo of foreign voices
booming from the mouths of mechanical instruments:
dragons setting ablaze with howls of grapeshot—
to the horror of my brothers
murdered in the night—
my bamboo houses
and my ancient pagodas

And now, from the airplane of my new conscience,
I watch over the green plains of Europe,
and her magnificent cities
blossoming in stone and iron.

Before my eyes the western world is naked.
With the long pipe of the centuries
in my pale hands,
I am no longer enticed by the opium of barbarism;
and today I march toward the progress of the people,
training my fingers on the trigger of a Mauser.

Over the flame of today
impatiently I cook the drug of tomorrow;
I would breathe deep of the new era
in my great pipe of jade.
A strange restlessness has taken all sleep from my
                                        slanting eyes.

To gain a deeper view of the horizon
I leap up on the old wall of the past . . .

Until yesterday I was polite and peaceful . . .

trans: Langston Hughes

NICOLÁS GUILLÉN, born in 1904 in Camaguey, Cuba, is the leader of the Afro-Cuban school of poetry. Vitier writes, "He is the only poet of this school for whom the Negro theme was neither a fashion nor simply a subject but the productive center of his whole creative activity." His collections of poetry include *Motivos de son* (1930), *Sóngoro cosongo* (1931), *West Indies Ltd.* (1937), and *Sones para turistas y cantos para soldados* (1937). An excellent translation of his poetry was made by Langston Hughes and Ben F. Carruthers entitled *Cuba Libre* (1948).

PROPOSITION

Tonight
when the moon comes out
I shall change it
into money.

But I'd be sorry
if people knew about it,
for the moon
is an old family treasure.

trans: Langston Hughes

GUADALUPE, W.I.

The Negroes, labouring
by the steamer. The Arabs,
hawking their wares,

the Frenchmen, strolling, taking it easy
and the sun, burning.

In the harbour the sea
lies at rest. The air
is scorching the palm-trees ...
I shout: "Guadalupe!" but no one answers.
The steamer departs,
ploughing the passive water to noisy spume.
Then, the Negroes
go on labouring,
the Arabs hawking their wares
the Frenchmen strolling and taking it easy
and the sun
burning.

trans: Anselm Hollo

DEAD SOLDIER

What bullet killed him?
　　Nobody knows.
Where was he born?
　　In Jovellanos, they say.
Why did they pick him up?
　　He was lying dead in the road.
　　And some other soldiers saw him.
What bullet killed him?

His sweetheart comes and kisses him.
His mother comes and cries.
When the Captain gets there
All he says is:
　　Bury him!

　　Rat-ta-tat-tat!
THERE GOES THE DEAD SOLDIER.

Rat-ta-tat-tat!
THEY PICKED HIM UP IN THE ROAD.

Rat-ta-tat-tat!
A SOLDIER AIN'T NOTHING.

Rat-ta-tat-tat!
THERE'RE PLENTY OF SOLDIERS.

trans: Langston Hughes

SIGHTSEERS IN A COURTYARD

Tourists in the courtyard
of an Havana tenement.
Cantaliso sings a song
not made for dancing.

Rather than your fine hotels,
stop in the courtyard of this tenement.
Here you'll see plenty of local color
you'll never find in your hotels.
Gentlemen, allow me to present to you
    Juan Concinero!
He owns one table and he owns one chair,
he owns one chair and he owns one table,
    and one oil stove.
The oil stove won't burn
and hasn't kissed a pot for ages.
But see how jolly and gay,
how well-fed and happy
    Juan Concinero
    is today!

Juan Concinero interrupts:
Folks, this is Louis, the candy-maker.
And this is Carlos from the Canaries.
And that Negro there is called Pedro Martinez.

And that other, Norberto Soto.
And that dark girl over there, Petra Sarda.
All of them live in the same room—
No doubt because that's not so dear.
What people! What high-class people live here!

All in chorus:
With what one tourist
spends on brandy in a day,
a month's room rent
anybody could pay.

The song goes on:
That woman coughing over there,
folks, by name of Juana:
tuberculosis in an advanced stage.
Nobody looked after her
so, like a dunce,
she went all day
without eating. A funny idea—
with so much food to waste!

All in chorus:
What one Yankee
drinks up with ease
Might've cured
Juana's disease.

The song ends:
Oh, but tourists, stay here,
and have a good time!
This is your chance!
Tourists, stay here!
Have a good time!
This is your chance!
I'll sing you songs
Nobody can dance!

trans: Langston Hughes

Panama

HERRERA S. DEMETRIO, born in Panama in 1902, is a mulatto who triumphed over extreme poverty by self-education. He has been described by critic Rodrigo Miró as "an ironical and intelligent spectator in the theatre of the world." His published works include *Mis primeros trinos* (1924), *Kodak* (1937), *La Fiesta de San Cristóbal* (1937), and *Los poemas del pueblo* (1939).

TRAINING

The sea——quick pugilist——
uses for a pun
        ching
            ball
the restless little boats.

With the towel of the wind,
even rubs down the boxer's
sweaty body.

The buildings——
ringside fans——
crowd close to watch
the big training.

(The dock is whispering
with a smoking ship . . .)

And the surf's applause
makes the tower stand on tiptoe

With its watch in hand
to keep the time.

Stray kids,
the sea-birds
sneak in through the roof.

trans: Dudley Fitts

Trinidad

HAROLD MILTON TELEMAQUE, born in 1911 at Plymouth, Tobago, Trinidad, is the son of a captain of a sailing schooner. He was educated by Moravian ministers at Bethesda after which he became a teacher. His published poetry includes *Burnt Bush* (1947).

ADINA

They hunt chameleon worlds with cameras.
Their guides avoid the virtue of our valleys,
They have not seen Adina's velvet figure
Swimming uncovered in our rivers' bubbles
They have not seen the bamboo's slow manoeuvre,
The light refracting round her shapely ankles:
They have not seen Adina's dancing beauty
Blazing effulgent in the Caribbean.

They stalk with telescopes the larger precincts
Their view ascends skyscrapers' hazy regions,
They have not seen the silver sun on green leaves,
Adina's basket starred with fruit and flowers,
The bird sung matinee, the dancing palm-trees,
Beside her rhythmic swinging arms
Storms do not strike
They have not seen Adina in the breezes
Blazing effulgent in the Caribbean.

St. Lucia

DEREK WALCOTT, born in 1930 in St. Lucia, Windward Islands, West Indies, has won many awards for his verse. He was chosen for the Guinness Award (1961) and a fellowship from the Rockefeller Foundation. His plays have been performed at the Royal Court Theatre in London and in Port of Spain, Trinidad, where he directs an important theatre group. His published poetry includes *In a Green Night* (1962) and *Selected Poems* (1964).

excerpt from A SEA-CHANTEY

Là, tout n'est qu'ordre et beauté,
Luxe, calme, et volupté.

In the middle of the harbour
A fish breaks the Sabbath
With a silvery leap.
The scales fall from him
In a tinkle of church-bells;
The town streets are orange
With the week-ripened sunlight,
Balanced on the bowsprit
A young sailor is playing
His grandfather's chantey
On a trembling mouth-organ
The music curls, dwindling
Like smoke from blue galleys,
To dissolve near the mountains.
The music uncurls with

The soft vowels of inlets,
The christening of vessels,
The titles of portages,
The colours of sea-grapes,
The tartness of sea-almonds,
The alphabet of church-bells,
The peace of white horses,
The pastures of ports,
The litany of islands,
The rosary of archipelagoes,
Anguilla, Antigua,
Virgin of Guadeloupe,
And stone-white Grenada
Of sunlight and pigeons,
The amen of calm waters,
The amen of calm waters,
The amen of calm waters.

MAN O'WAR BIRD

The idling pivot of the frigate bird
Sways the world's scales, tilts cobalt sea and sky,
Rightens, by a round eye, my drift
Through heaven if I shift
My study of the sun.
                         The easy wings
Depend upon the stress I give to things
Like my importance to its piercing height, the peace
Of its slow, ravening circuit of a speck
Upon a beach prey to its beak
Like any predatory tern it seizes.
In that blue wildfire somewhere is an Eye
That weighs the world exactly as it pleases.

THE WHALE, HIS BULWARK

To praise the blue whale's crystal jet,
To write, O fountain, honouring a spout,
Provokes this curse:
                    "The high are humbled yet,"
From times that humble Godhead, beasthood, verse.

Once the Lord raised his bulwark to our eyes,
Once, in these seas, whales threshed,
The harpooner was common. Once, I heard
Of a baleine beached up the Grenadines, fleshed
By excited, antlike villagers a prize
Reduced from majesty to pigmy-size,
Salt-crusted, mythological,
And dead.

The boy who told me couldn't believe his eyes,
And I believed him. When I was small,
God and a foundered whale were possible.
Whales are rarer, God as invisible.
Yet, through his gift, I praise the unfathomable,
Though the boy may be dead, the praise unfashionable,
The tale apocryphal.

NEARING LA GUAIRA

At dead of night, the sailors sprawled on deck.
The wind shakes out its blanket overhead.
All are ribbed equally; all must shipwreck.
The breakers kiss, then bitterly separate,
There is one error flesh cannot repent
Nor motion drown, not while one moon makes white
The tossed sea and her sheet's dishevellment.

Like men in graves, each disappointing west,
They wait in patience for the coming east;

Farewell to that, I have made my separate peace,
Bitter and sleepless as the ocean's curse.
A sailor in an oil-stained vest looks down
To the sea's lace, ripped by the raging wind.
"Buenas noches, amigo, qué tal?"
"Nada, amigo, nada."
The stars fly from his cigarette in the wind.
A broken man, with a dead wife in mind.
"Mañana esaremos en La Guaira."
I ask him what La Guaira means, he grins,
Says it means nothing.

So, the next morning, nothing is green water,
Sun to the left like a starfish, the moon a washed-out shell
And on rust hills, La Guaira, strict as sorrow.
And nothing is a cornet in the plaza, nothing the Morro
Where the garbage drifts, nothing
The bullfight roaring for six thousand tickets,
Nothing Christ's blood forgotten
In the arena of the free cathedral.
Nothing the soldiers drilling in the square,
And the green fountain with its sacrament.
Señor, we have joined a different detachment.

Nothing her mouth, my east and crimson west,
Nothing our restless, separated sleep;
Nothing is bitter and is very deep.

A FAR CRY FROM AFRICA

A wind is ruffling the tawny pelt
Of Africa. Kikuyu, quick as flies,
Batten upon the bloodstreams of the veldt.
Corpses are scattered through a paradise.
Only the worm, colonel of carrion, cries:
"Waste no compassion on these separate dead!"

Statistics justify and scholars seize
The salients of colonial policy.
What is that to the white child hacked in bed?
To savages, expendable as Jews?

Threshed out by beaters, the long rushes break
In a white dust of ibises whose cries
Have wheeled since civilization's dawn
From the parched river or beast-teeming plain.
The violence of beast on beast is read
As natural law, but upright man
Seeks his divinity by inflicting pain.
Delirious as these worried beasts, his wars
Dance to the tightened carcass of a drum,
While he calls courage still that native dread
Of the white peace contracted by the dead.

Again brutish necessity wipes its hands
Upon the napkin of a dirty cause, again
A waste of our compassion, as with Spain,
The gorilla wrestles with the superman.

I who am poisoned with the blood of both,
Where shall I turn, divided to the vein?
I who have cursed
The drunken officer of British rule, how choose
Between this Africa and the English tongue I love?
Betray them both, or give back what they give?
How can I face such slaughter and be cool?
How can I turn from Africa and live?

Jamaica

WALTER ADOLPHE ROBERTS, born in 1886 in Kingston, Jamaica, has spent most of his life in the United States where he has been active as a poet, journalist, novelist, and biographer. During World War I he was war correspondent for the *Brooklyn Eagle* and he served as editor of *Ainslee's Magazine* and associate editor of *Hearst's International Magazine*. His books include novels, biographies, historical works, and two books of verse entitled *Pierrot Wounded and Other Poems* (1919) and *Pan and Peacocks* (1938).

ON A MONUMENT TO MARTÍ

Cuba, disheveled, naked to the waist,
Springs up erect from the dark earth and screams
Her joy in liberty. The metal gleams
Where her chains broke. Magnificent her haste
To charge into the battle and to taste
Revenge on the oppressor. Thus she seems.
But she were powerless without the dreams
Of him who stands above, unsmiling, chaste.

Yes, over Cuba on her jubilant way
Broods the Apostle, José Julian Martí.
He shaped her course of glory, and the day
The guns first spoke he died to make her free.
That night a meteor flamed in splendid loss
Between the North Star and the Southern Cross.

AGNES MAXWELL-HALL, born in 1894 in Montego Bay, Jamaica, was educated in London, Boston, and New York City where she studied short-story writing at Columbia University. Besides writing, she operates and owns a dairy in the Jamaican mountains at Kempshot. Her poetry appears in such anthologies as *The Poetry of the Negro.*

JAMAICA MARKET

Honey, pepper, leaf-green limes,
Pagan fruit whose names are rhymes,
Mangoes, breadfruit, ginger-roots,
Granadillas, bamboo-shoots,
Cho-cho, ackees, tangerines,
Lemons, purple Congo-beans,
Sugar, okras, kola-nuts,
Citrons, hairy coconuts,
Fish, tobacco, native hats,
Gold bananas, woven mats,
Plantains, wild-thyme, pallid leeks,
Pigeons with their scarlet beaks,
Oranges and saffron yams,
Baskets, ruby guava jams,
Turtles, goat-skins, cinnamon,
Allspice, conch-shells, golden rum.
Black skins, babel—and the sun
That burns all colours into one.

CLAUDE McKAY (1891–1948), born in Jamaica, gained world recognition when in World War II Sir Winston Churchill read his sonnet "If We Must Die" in the House of Commons. At the age of sixteen, he met Walter Jekyll, a specialist in Jamaican folklore, who taught McKay how to use native dialect in his first poems. Among his many travels, he went to Russia and met Lenin and Trotsky and addressed the Third Internationale. He served as an associate editor of *The Liberator* and *The Masses*. He wrote poetry, novels, autobiographies, and a sociological study entitled *Harlem: Negro Metropolis* (1940). His published poetry includes *Songs of Jamaica* (1911), *Spring in New Hampshire* (1920), *Harlem Shadows* (1922), and *Selected Poems* (1953).

THE TROPICS IN NEW YORK

Bananas ripe and green, and ginger-root,
Cocoa in pods and alligator pears,
And tangerines and mangoes and grapefruit,
Fit for the highest prize at parish fairs,

Set in the window, bringing memories
Of fruit-trees laden by low-singing rills,
And dewy dawns, and mystical blue skies
In benediction over nun-like hills.

My eyes grew dim, and I could no more gaze;
A wave of longing through my body swept,
And, hungry for the old, familiar ways,
I turned aside and bowed my head and wept.

IF WE MUST DIE

If we must die, let it not be like hogs
Hunted and penned in an inglorious spot,
While round us bark the mad and hungry dogs,
Making their mock at our accursed lot.

If we must die, O let us nobly die,
So that our precious blood may not be shed
In vain; then even the monsters we defy
Shall be constrained to honor us though dead!
O kinsmen! we must meet the common foe!
Though far outnumbered let us show us brave,
And for their thousand blows deal one deathblow!
What though before us lies the open grave?
Like men we'll face the murderous, cowardly pack,
Pressed to the wall, dying, but fighting back!

AMERICA

Although she feeds me bread of bitterness,
And sinks into my throat her tiger's tooth,
Stealing my breath of life, I will confess
I love this cultured hell that tests my youth!
Her vigor flows like tides into my blood,
Giving me strength erect against her hate.
Her bigness sweeps my being like a flood.
Yet as a rebel fronts a king in state,
I stand within her walls with not a shred
Of terror, malice, not a word of jeer.
Darkly I gaze into the days ahead,
And see her might and granite wonders there,
Beneath the touch of Time's unerring hand,
Like priceless treasures sinking in the sand.

French Guiana

LÉON DAMAS, born in 1912 in French Guiana, is one of the leaders of the Negritude movement. In his youth he went to Paris where he became a protege of André Gide and friend of the surrealist André Breton. At one time he was elected a deputy to the French National Assembly. His published poetry includes *Graffiti* (1952), *Black-Label* (1956), *Pigments* (1962), *Nevralgies* (1966), and in English translation *African songs of love, war, grief and abuse* (1961).

THEY CAME THIS EVENING

They came this evening where the
    tom
        tom
            rolled with
                rhythm in
                    rhythm
                        the frenzy
of eyes
the frenzy of hands the frenzy
of feet of statues
SINCE
how many SELVES
have died
since they came this evening where the
    tom
        tom

                    rolled with
                        rhythm in
                            rhythm
                                the frenzy
of eyes
the frenzy of hands the frenzy
of feet of statues.

                              trans: Seth L. Wolitz

        PUT DOWN

I feel ridiculous
in their shoes in their dinner jackets
in their shirts in their detachable collars
in their monocles in their bowler hats
I feel ridiculous
with my toes which were not made to
perspire from morning to night
with wrappings which weaken the limbs
and take away from my body its beauty of hidden sex

I feel ridiculous with my neck in the smoke stack
with these headaches which cease
each time I bow to someone

I feel ridiculous
in their drawing rooms in their manners
in their bows in their formulas
in their manifold needs of apish antics

I feel ridiculous
with all they relate
until they serve you in the afternoon a bit of hot water
and sickly cakes

I feel ridiculous
with the theories they season
to the taste of their needs of their passions

of their instincts revealed in the night in form of a doormat
I feel ridiculous
among them an accomplice among them a pimp
among them a butcher with hands frightfully red
with the blood of their civilization.

trans: Seth L. Wolitz

Martinique

AIMÉ CÉSAIRE, born in 1913 in Martinique, is considered the outstanding poet of the Negritude movement. He attended the Ecole Normale Supérieure de Paris and returned to his native island where he taught literature, served as representative to two national legislative assemblies of France, was mayor of Fort-de-France and Consul General. He returned to France to be Representative from Martinique in the French Assembly. Among his many books of published verse is a bilingual edition of *Cahier d'un retour au pays natal* (1947).

from RETURN TO MY NATIVE LAND

I shall not regard my swelled head as a sign of real glory.

And I laugh at my old puerile dreams.

No, we have never been amazons of the king of Dahomey, nor princes of Ghana with eight hundred camels, nor wise men in Timbuctoo under Askia the Great; nor architects in Djene, nor mahdis, nor warriors. Under our armpits, we do not feel the itch of those who bore the lance. And since I have sworn to hide nothing of our history (I who admire nothing so much as the lamb chewing his afternoon shadow), I want to declare that we were from the very first quite pitiful dishwashers, shoeshiners without scope, and, at best, rather conscientious sorcerers whose only incontestable achievement has been the endurance record under the lash.

And this country cried for centuries that we were stupid brutes; that the pulsations of humanity stopped before the doors of the slave compound; that we are a walking dunghill, hideously promising sweet sugar-canes and silky cotton, and they branded us with red-hot irons and we slept in our excrement and they sold us on the market for less than an ell of English cloth, and the salted meat from Ireland was cheaper than we, and this country was calm, tranquil, and was convinced that it acted in accordance with the will of God.

> We the vomit of slavers
> we the venery of the Calebars
> what? that we should stuff our ears?
> We, made dead drunk with the ship's rolling,
> with jeers, with the sea-fog inhaled!
> Forgive us, whirlpool our accomplice!

I hear from the hold below the curses of the chained, the hiccups of the dying, the splash of someone thrown into the sea . . . the baying of a woman in labour . . . the scraping of nails seeking throats . . . the chuckles of the whip . . . the scurrying of vermin across worn-out bodies . . .

.   .   .   .

> I accept . . . I accept . . . totally, without reserve . . .
> my race which no ablution of hyssop or mixed lilies
> could purify
> my race eaten by macula
> my race ripe grape for drunken feet
> my queen of spittle and lepers
> my queen of whips and scrofula
> my queen of squasms and chloasms
> (o these queens that I used to love in the far spring gardens behind the illumination of all the candles of the chestnut-trees!)

I accept. I accept.
And the flogged Negro who says: "Pardon, my master"
and the twenty-nine blows of the legal whip
and the cell four feet high
and the spiked iron collar
and my runaway audacity hamstrung
and the *fleur de lys* which flows from the red iron on
the fat of my shoulder
and the kennel of Monsieur VAULTIER MAYES-
COURT, where I barked six months like a poodle
and Monsieur BRAFIN
and Monsieur DE FOURNIOL
and Monsieur DE LA MAHAUDIÉRE
and the yaws
and the mastiff
the suicide
the promiscuity
the half-boot
the stock
the wooden horse
the turnscrew
the whip-cord
See, am I humble enough? Have I enough calluses on
my knees? muscles on my kidneys?
Crawl in the mud. Brace oneself in the fat of the mud.
Carry. Soil of mud. Horizon of mud. Sky of mud.

.   .   .   .

And we are standing now, my country and I, hair in
the wind, my little hand now in its enormous fist, and force
is not in us, but above us, in a voice which pierces the night
and the audience like the sting of an apocalyptic hornet.
And the voice declares that for centuries Europe has
stuffed us with lies and bloated us with pestilence,
for it is not true that the work of man is finished

that we have nothing to do in the world
that we are parasites in the world
that we have only to accept the way of the world
but the work of man has only begun

and it remains for man to conquer all prohibitions immobilized in the corners of his fervor

and no race has a monopoly of beauty, intelligence, strength

and there is room for all at the rendezvous of conquest and we know that the sun turns around our earth, lighting only the portion that our single will has fixed and that every star falls from sky to earth at our limitless command . . .

.   .   .   .

In vain to distract himself the captain hangs to his yardarm the lustiest Negro or hurls him in the sea or turns his dogs on him

the "poor-old-Negro" with the smell of fried onion finds again in his spilled blood the bitter taste of liberty

And the "poor-old-Negro" is standing up
the seated "poor-old-Negro"
unexpectedly standing
upright in the hold
upright in the cabins
upright on the bridge
upright in the wind
upright under the sun
upright in the blood
   upright
      and
         free
and the lustral ship advances unafraid on the crumbling water . . .

trans: Emile Snyders

MODERN AFRICA

This chapter is but a foretaste of some great encyclo-
pedia of black poetry to come, for it deals only with the work
of those modern African bards who have learned to write in
English, French, and Portuguese. Meanwhile, the poetry in a
thousand vernaculars remains unknown. What we know
about this vast jungle of song is due to one or two basic publications and to the sifting of one or two devoted editors—to
Présence Africaine in French and *Black Orpheus* in English
and to the creative criticism and the pioneering publications of
Ulli Beier, Jahnheinz Jahn, and Gerald Moore. Them we
thank.

In Africa the poet has always been a hero, sometimes more
feared than kings. The very gods are summoned and dis-
missed with song in all West Africa. The songs of the min-
strels of the Hausa tribe can bring down the king in ridicule,
since the satire of the poet can so wound a man that he will go
into exile or lose his taste for life. This is because in the old
Africa poems are not arrangements of words to be read in
the silence of a room, but songs to be sung loud and strong
in public places—and not only songs but dances. The words
of poems have a magic meaning—they do not merely symbol-
ize the thing or the person they evoke—they *are* the person

and the thing. This magical effect is enhanced by the playful vocal skill of the bard, who applies his voice like a lash, a stinging nettle, a serpent's bite, a caress, or a trickle of cool water. The song is also danced out and dramatized in mimicry so irresistible that it sets the whole tribe, the whole confederacy, the whole world humming and dancing, laughing or lamenting. So the hunter praised or the great man pilloried can never escape the sound of himself.

The *griots,* the native poets, of Senegal are modern Davids who still perform prodigies upon great lyres, like those played before the pharoahs and the kings of Judah. No wonder, then, that Senegal gave birth to the first poets of the *nègritude* school—Leopold Senghor and David Diop, who, as young men, encountered Aimé Césaire in Paris in the thirties. All three had obtained the best French education; they were received in the best French society; their work was praised by the cream of French intellectuals, but they refused to be assimilated. They resolved upon a total spiritual return to their own culture.

Césaire set down his resolve in flaming lines of the book-length poem *Notes on a Return to My Country.* Léopold Senghor could sing more coolly. As an African he had only to look over his shoulder and out into any night in his own village to find a rich ancestry. His poetry develops the main themes of the school of *nègritude*—the presence of the protecting and beneficent dead, the beauty of African women, of night and of sleep—the harsh rigidity of the white and a yearning for the humanity of African culture—the devastation of black civilization by whites and a call to blacks to resist. Like the first African songs, like the blues, Senghor's flowing lines magically evoke Africa out of its long silence by the use of rich imagery, but, even more, by setting verse to African rhythms. Jahn tells how the Senegalese innovator experimented with streams of phonemes and complex systems of accent to evoke the feel of dancing and the sound of drumming in his poetry. Senghor, himself, has said:

"A poem is like a passage of jazz, where the execution is just as important as the text . . . I still think that a poem is not complete until it is sung, words and music together."

A far more bitter irony characterizes the work of the younger Senegalese poet, David Diop, who speaks of the days when

> . . . civilization kicked us in the face,
> When holy water slapped our cringing brows.

The French-speaking poets of the Cameroons and of the Ivory Coast of Dahomey and the Congo continued the themes of nègritude.

> For having created me black, I give you thanks O God.
> White is a color for an occasion
> Black the color of all days.
> And I carry the world since the morning of time.

A school of African poets writing in English grew up around the University of Ibadan in Nigeria, where the review *Black Orpheus* was founded to publish their work. These British colonial blacks were not struggling against assimilation, since the British had no self-conscious cultural policy. As a new generation of poets, born twenty years after Césaire and Senghor, they felt some animosity to their precursors. They expressed amusement at the concept of nègritude. "A tiger does not just proclaim his tigritude," says one, "he pounces." Yet on the whole, these new poets continued in the vein established by Senghor and Césaire. Said Gabriel Okara:

> The mystic drum beat in my inside.
> The fishes danced in the rivers.
> The men and women danced on land
> To the rhythm of my drum.

Another poet announced:

> I struck tomorrow square in the face.
> Yesterday groaned and said,
> Please mind your steps today.

In spite of rapid political change, these young black rebels had to deal with the racial problem. Wole Soyinka reports on the problem of an African hunting a room in London, talking on the telephone to a lily-white landlady:

> *Facially, I am brunette, but madam, you should see*
> *the rest of me. Palms of my hand, soles of my feet*
> *are a peroxide blond. Friction caused—*
> *foolishly, madam—by sitting down, has turned*
> *my bottom raven black— One moment madam!—sensing*
> *her receiver rearing on the thunderclap*
> *about my ears—"Madam," I pleaded, "wouldn't you rather*
> *see for yourself?"*

Black poets had developed much earlier among the southern Bantu in South Africa, where the mission stations provided an education for talented young men and encouraged them to write in their own languages. Black writers began to turn out excellent work in the Sotho, Zhosa, and Zulu tongues. Their fiction often concerned the struggle of the Bantus in adapting to white culture. The best of the poetry celebrated the ancient glories of the Bantu past, as in the poem on page 173 which praises Mohesh, the wily chieftain who defeated the best troops Britain could send against him. The poets here continue the role of their bardic ancestors. Even Christian hymns were composed in praise song style. Today the mood has changed, as evidenced in a praise song by a modern South African poet:

> *The devil is good and friendly.*
> *that's what he's the Son of God for.*
> *he's the first, the very first, king.*
> *he was made from hard stone.*
> *he is created out of ore ...*

The irony of these lines reflects the present situation of the black writer in South Africa. The land of *apartheid* has no place for even so mild a protest as *On the Gold Mines* (see p. 176). The Nationalist party abolished the mission schools, censored the native literature, and drove the best writers into exile. The poetry that is permitted is poor stuff, but one may imagine that there are songs and singers hidden away from the sight of the police which keep alive the fiery spirit of the Zulus. The songs of Miriam Makeba are evidence for that . . .

If the source were not Africa—the continent preeminent of dance and song and poetry—it would be hard to believe that so much fine verse could have been produced under such adverse circumstances and in the span of three generations this anthology covers. Most that is printed in these pages from Africa was written by poets who had to learn a European language and absorb exotic literary conventions before they could begin. Most of these poems have suffered from at least one stage of translation. Portuguese-speaking poets live in the stifling atmosphere produced by a reactionary colonial regime. The leading poet of Angola is in hiding after an escape from a Portuguese prison. Portuguese Africa is still a colony, with all that this implies for its black intellectuals. Cavierinha writes:

> *I come from somewhere.*
> *From a small nation that does not yet exist.*
> *I came and I am here . . .*
> *I have a heart*
> *And cries which are not mine alone*
> *I come from a country which does not yet exist.*

These poets return again and again to the praise of black women:

> *Black mother rocks her son*
> *And in her black head covered with black hair*

She keeps marvelous dreams ...
She dreams of marvelous worlds,
Marvelous worlds
Where her son will be able to live.

The anguish in the lines of these poets in the Portuguese colonies recalls the recent past when Europe was subject to an aristocratic tyranny that knew no bounds because of its inherited, its god-given, right to rule.

For you tormentors,
forgiveness has no name.
Justice shall be heard.
And the blood of lives fallen
in the forests of death,
innocent blood
drenching the earth
shall make the earth fruitful,
crying for justice.

Senegal

LÉOPOLD SÉDAR SENGHOR, born in 1906 at Joal in Senegal, is not only the President of his country, but also one of the leaders of the "négritude" literary movement. The best known of his works are *Selected Poems of Senghor* (translated by John Reed and Clive Wake), *Chants e'ombre* (1956), *Chants pour Naëtt* (1949), *Ethiopiques* (1956), *Nocturnes* (1961). He edited the definitive anthology of African poetry, *La Nouvelle Poésie nègre et malgache*.

WE DELIGHTED, MY FRIEND

We delighted, my friend, in an African presence:
Furniture from Guinea and the Congo,
Heavy and polished, dark and light.
Primitive and pure masks on distant walls yet so near.
Taborets of honor for the hereditary hosts,
The princes from the high country.
Wild and proud perfumes from the thick tresses of silence,
Cushions of shadow and leisure like quiet wells running.
Eternal words and the distant alternating chant
As in the loin cloth from the Sudan.
But then the friendly light of your blue kindness
Will soften the obsession of this presence in
Black, white, and red, O red like the soil of Africa.

trans: Miriam Koshland

ON THE APPEAL FROM THE RACE
OF SHEBA: II

Bless you, Mother.
I remember the days of my fathers, the evenings of Dyilor
That deep-blue light of the night sky on the land sweet
                                        at evening.
Sitting on the steps of the dwelling deep in shadow,
My brothers and sisters clustering round my heart with
                                    the warmth of chicks,
My head resting on the lap of my nurse Nga, Nga the poetess,
My head humming with the war-like gallop of the dyoung,
            dyoungs, the gallop of my pure thoroughbred blood
My head singing with the distant plaintive melodies of
                                        Koumba the orphan.
In the centre of the courtyard, the solitary fig tree
And amongst the moonlit shadows the wives of Man
            chatted with voices as deep as their eyes and as the
                                nocturnal fountains of Fimla.
My father stretched out on peaceful mats, but big, but
                                    strong, but handsome
Man of the Kingdom of Sine; whilst all around the
            passionate fingers of the *griots* danced over the *koras*,
                                sounding a heroic song
Whereas from further afield, heavy with strong warm
            odours, came the classical murmurous movement of a
                                    hundred herds.

                                trans: John Reed and Clive Wake

BLACK WOMAN

Naked woman, black woman
Clad in your color that is life, in your form that is beauty!
I have grown up in your shade, the sweetness of your hands
                                    bound my eyes.
And now in the heart of summer and noon, I discover you,

promised earth, from the tower of your sun-scorched
                                                              neck
And your beauty smites me to the full of my heart like the
                                              flash of an eagle.

Naked woman, dark woman!
Firm-fleshed ripe fruit, dark raptures of black wine, mouth
                                      making lyric my mouth
Savanna of sheer horizons, savanna quivering to the East
                                    wind's fervent caresses
Carved tom-tom, taut tom-tom snarling under the Victor's
                                        fingers
Your grave, contralto voice is the spiritual of the Beloved.

Naked woman, dark woman!
Oil sweet and smooth on the athlete's flanks,
On the flanks of the princes of Mali
Heaven-leased gazelle, pearls are stars on the night
                                      of your skin
Delights of the spirit at play, red gold reflections
                                  on your shimmering skin.
In the shade of your hair, my anguish lightens with the
                                 nearing suns of your eyes.

Naked woman, black woman!
I sing your passing beauty, form that I fix in the eternal
Before jealous destiny burns you to ashes to nourish
                                 the roots of life.

trans: Anne Atik

PRAYER FOR PEACE: II

For grand organ

Lord, God, forgive white Europe.
It is true Lord, that for four enlightened centuries, she
                    has scattered the baying and slaver of her mastiffs
                                over my lands

And the Christians, forsaking Thy light and the gentleness
                    of Thy heart
Have lit their camp fires with my parchments, tortured my
        disciples, deported my doctors and masters of science.
Their powder has crumbled in a flash the pride of *tatas*
                    and hills
And their bullets have gone through the bowels of vast
        empires like daylight, from the Horn of the West to
                    the Eastern Horizon
They have fired the intangible woods like hunting grounds,
        dragged out Ancestors and spirits by their peaceable
                    beards,
And turned their mystery into Sunday distraction for
                    somnambulent bourgeois.
Lord, forgive them who turned the Askia into *maquisards*,
                    my princes into sergeant-majors
My household servants into 'boys,' my peasants into
            wage-earners, my people into a working class.
For Thou must forgive those who have hunted my
                    children like wild elephants,
And broken them in with whips, have made them the
                black hands of those whose hands were white.
For Thou must forget those who exported ten millions
                of my sons in the leperhouses of their ships
Who killed two hundred millions of them.
And have made for me a solitary old age in the forest
                of my nights and the savanna of my days.
Lord, the glasses of my eyes grow dim
And lo, the serpent of hatred raises its head in my heart,
                that serpent that I believed was dead.

                    trans: John Reed and Clive Wake

DAVID DIOP (1927–60), born in Bordeaux, lived most of his life as a semi-invalid in France. He died in an air crash near Dakar, Senegal, with the manuscript of his second book of poems. His first volume *Coups de Pilon* (1956) was published by *Présence Africaine*.

AFRICA

Africa, my Africa,
Africa of proud warriors
In ancestral savannas,
Africa of whom my grandmother sings,
On the banks of the distant river
I have never known you
But your blood flows in my veins
Your beautiful black blood
That irrigates the fields
The blood of your sweat
The work of your slavery
The slavery of your children.
Africa, tell me, Africa,
Is this you, this back that is bent,
This back that breaks
Under the weight of humiliation
This back trembling with red scars
Saying *yes* to the whip under the midday sun?
A grave voice answers me:
Impetuous son, this tree, young and strong,
This tree there in splendid isolation
Amidst white and faded flowers,
That is Africa, your Africa,
That grows again, patiently, obstinately
As its fruit gradually acquires
The bitter taste of liberty.

trans: Ulli Beier

HE WHO HAS LOST ALL

The sun shone in my hut
And my wives were fair and supple
Like the palms in the night breeze.
My children passed over the wide river
Deep as death
And my canoes vied with the crocodiles.
The motherly moon attended our dances
The wild and heavy rhythm of the tom-tom,
Tom-tom of joy, tom-tom of recklessness
      Midst fires of freedom.

Then one day, the Silence . . .
The sun's rays seemed to die out
In my hut empty of meaning.
My wives crushed their reddened mouths
Against the thin hard lips of steel-eyed conquerors
And my children left their calm nudity
For the uniform of iron and blood.
Your voice, too, died out.
The irons of slavery have rent my heart
Tom-toms of my nights, tom-toms of my fathers.

trans: Anne Atik

THE VULTURES

In those days
When civilization kicked us in the face
When holy water slapped our cringing brows
The vultures built in the shadow of their talons
The bloodstained monument of tutelage.
In those days
There was painful laughter on the metallic hell of the roads
And the monotonous rhythm of the paternoster
Drowned the howling on the plantations.

O the bitter memories of extorted kisses
Of promises broken at the point of a gun
Of foreigners who did not seem human
Who knew all the books but did not know love.
But we whose hands fertilize the womb of the earth
In spite of your songs of pride
In spite of the desolate villages of torn Africa
Hope was preserved in us as in a fortress
And from the mines of Swaziland to the factories of Europe
Spring will be reborn under our bright steps.

trans: Ulli Beier

BIRAGO DIOP, born in 1906 at Dakar, Senegal, studied at
Lycée Faidherbe in St. Louis and later became a government vet-
erinary officer. His interest in folklore has led him to publish several collections of folk tales. His published volumes of poetry
include *Leurres et lueurs* (1960), *Les Contes d'Amadou Koumba*
(1947), *Les Nouveaux Contes d'Amadou Koumba* (1958).

BREATHS

Listen more often
To things than to beings;
The fire's voice is heard,
Hear the voice of water.
Hear in the wind
The bush sob:
It is the ancestors' breath.

Those who died have never left,
They are in the brightening shadow
And in the thickening shadow;
The dead are not under earth,
They are in the rustling tree,

They are in the groaning woods,
They are in the flowing water,
They are in the still water,
They are in the hut, they are in the crowd:
The dead are not dead.

Listen more often
To things than to beings;
The fire's voice is heard,
Hear the voice of water.
Hear in the wind
The bush sob:
It is the ancestors' breath.
The breath of dead ancestors
Who have not left,
Who are not under earth,
Who are not dead.
Those who died have never left,
They are in the woman's breast,
They are in the wailing child
And in the kindling firebrand.
The dead are not under earth,
They are in the fire dying down,
They are in the moaning rock,
They are in the crying grass,
They are in the forest, they are in the home:
The dead are not dead.

Listen more often
To things than to beings,
The fire's voice is heard,
Hear the voice of water.
Hear in the wind
The bush sob:
It is the ancestors' breath.

Each day it repeats the pact,
The great pact which binds,
Which binds our fate to the law;
Acts, to stronger breaths
The fate of our dead not dead;
The heavy pact which ties us to life,
The heavy law which binds us to acts
Breaths dying
In bed and on river banks,
Breaths which stir
In the moaning rock and crying grass.
Breaths which lodge
In the shadow brightening or thickening,
In the rustling tree, in the groaning woods,
And in the flowing water, and in the still water,
Breaths much stronger,
Breaths which have taken
The breath of the dead not dead,
The dead who have not left,
The dead no longer under earth.

Listen more often
To things than to beings;
The fire's voice is heard,
Hear the voice of water.
Hear in the wind
The bush sob:
It is the ancestors' breath.

                              trans: Anne Atik

Cameroun

MBELLA SONNE DIPOKO, born in 1936 in Duala, Cameroon, was educated in Cameroon and in Nigeria. He has worked in the Nigerian Broadcasting Corporation as a news reporter and is now living in France. Many of his poems have been published in *Présence Africaine*. His novel *A Few Nights and Days*, the first of a triology, was published in 1966.

AUTOBIOGRAPHY

We crawled and cried and laughed
Without hope
Without despair.
We grew up
Fenced in by the forest.
But this world of uncles and fathers and mothers and others—
Our fine world of greenness and grins was blown away
By the terrible storm of growth
And the mind soon flung pebbles at the cranes of the off-shore
island.

But today
Floods flee the rising sun
And owls hoot from the edge of the dark song.
Like cripples blinded by sandy winds
Dreams drift under the low sky of our sleep
And our hearts listen to the voice of days in flight
Our thoughts dusting the past.

Ivory Coast

BERNARD DADIÉ, born in 1916 at Assinie in the Ivory Coast, became interested in African folklore and traditions while working at a museum in Dakar (Senegal). Since then he has returned home to the Ivory Coast, where he has written two novels, collections of African folklore, and a volume of poetry, *La Ronde des jours* (1956).

DRY YOUR TEARS, AFRICA!

Dry your tears, Africa!
Your children come back to you
Out of the storm and squalls of fruitless journeys.

Through the crest of the wave and the babbling of the breeze,
Over the gold of the east
and the purple of the setting sun,
the peaks of the proud mountains
and the grasslands drenched with light
They return to you
out of the storm and squalls of fruitless journeys.

Dry your tears, Africa!
We have drunk
From all the springs
    of ill fortune
    and of glory.

And our senses are now opened
    to the splendour of your beauty

to the smell of your forests
to the charm of your waters
to the clearness of your skies
to the caress of your sun
And to the charm of your foliage pearled by the dew.

Dry your tears, Africa!
Your children come back to you
their hands full of playthings
and their hearts full of love.
They return to clothe you
in their dreams and their hopes.

trans: Donatus Ibe Nwoga

I GIVE YOU THANKS MY GOD

I give you thanks my God for having created me black,
For having made me
The total of all sorrows,
and set upon my head
the World.
I wear the livery of the Centaur
And I carry the World since the first morning.

White is a colour improvised for an occasion
Black, the colour of all days
And I carry the World since the first night.

I am happy
with the shape of my head
fashioned to carry the World,
satisfied with the shape of my nose,
Which should breathe all the air of the World,
happy
with the form of my legs
prepared to run through all the stages of the World.

I give you thanks my God, for having created me black,
for having made of me
the total of all sorrows.
Thirty-six swords have pierced my heart.
Thirty-six brands have burned my body,
And my blood on all the calvaries has reddened the snow,
And my blood from all the east has reddened nature.
And yet I am
Happy to carry the World,
Content with my short arms,
with my long legs,
with the thickness of my lips.

I give you thanks my God, for having created me black,
White is a colour for an occasion,
Black the colour of all days
And I carry the World since the morning of time.
And my laughter in the night brought forth day over the
                                                    World.
I give you thanks my God for having created me black.

trans: Donatus Ibe Nwoga

Dahomey

PAULIN JOACHIM was born in 1931 in Cotonou, Dahomey. He was awarded a diploma in journalism at L'Ecole Supérieure de Journalisme in Paris and was at one time political editor of France-Soir. He has published a volume of verse, *Un Nègre raconte*.

BURIAL

Because time subdues sharp angles and closes wounds
I want to forget the bare and baneful time of the first ages
the time of silver nitrate corrosive and bone-destroying
the time of our breakdown between the navel and history
with the needle flickering crazily at zero hour
the time of the inarticulate prayer
of simulated life and of the shame of being stretched out to
                                        the point of stupefaction
the time when we were affiliated to poverty
as one is connected to the gas or electricity supply
the time when eternity was turned inside out and the spectre
            of death no longer even gnawed at our minds
the time when I was aggressively healthy under the solar
                                        inflation
the time of tears and impatience
the time of the sleepwalker
the time when we were forced to invent
a third ear with which to listen
to what is not said by the rod of time

by the baleful power suspended over our heads
to which has been given a mandate from all eternity to break
our backs

But because time heals those wounds and softens angles
I wish to rear up a monolith to time
I ejected by time and exiled by former ages
now reintegrate time
and become its sacred aorta
see how my territory widens
my land of shadows awakening hollowing itself out
like a limitless reservoir for the ages to come.

trans: Oliver Bernard

Congo

EMMANUEL BOUNDZEKEI-DONGALA. No biographical in-formation was available at the time of publication.

FANTASY UNDER THE MOON

(Blues for a muted trumpet)

I climbed towards you on a ray of moonlight
that filtered through a hole in my straw-thatched house
When I had reached the smiling arch of your mouth among
the stars
you came to me
open under the sea of your body the heaving wave under
my body
my heart beating to the rhythm of yours moving to the
rhythm of your tribe the people of the mountain;
your serpent form writhing beneath mine
I sucked your cobra's poison from your broken lips
and my fever mounted like a sickness.

I visited last night our banana grove of the first time.
When I reached those great sombre aisles
under which we pressed each other beyond your mother's
knowledge
under the teasing trumpet of thirsty mosquitoes
the circle of my arms about your shadow your phantom

all at once hung emptier than the rope of a wine-tapper
embracing the palm tree.

I don't know why that large cloud crossing the moon
suddenly made the tide of your body fall.
Like oiled wrestlers at a festival
who feel their adversary slide between their arms
powerless I felt you slip from mine
under the moon's light white as this wine as your teeth
                                    which made you so gay
as you fluttered wildly in the circle of the dance
while your mother warned you not to come near me.

I looked up at the sky from the depths of my hut;
the moon was only a smile, your white smile congealed.

trans: Gerald Moore & Ulli Beier

TCHICAYA U TAM'SI, born in 1931 at Mpili in the Middle
Congo, has contributed to various French reviews in Paris where
he now lives. His books of poetry include *Le Mauvais Sang*
(1955), *Feu de brousse* (1957), *A Triche-Couer* (1960), *Épitomé*
(1962), *Le Ventre* (1965), and an English translation of *Feu de
brousse* ("Brush Fire") (1964).

THE SCORNER

I drink to your glory my god
You who have made me so sad
You have given me a people who are not distillers of gin

What wine shall I drink to your jubilate
In this country which has no vines
In this desert all the bushes are of cactus
Shall I take their crop of flowers

for flames of the burning bush of your desire
Tell me in what Egypt my people's feet lie chained

Christ I laugh at your sadness
O my sweet Christ
Thorn for thorn
We have a common crown of thorns
I will be converted because you tempt me
Joseph comes to me
I suck already the breast of the Virgin your mother
I count more than your one Judas on my fingers
My eyes lie to my soul
Where the world is a lamb your pascal lamb—Christ
I will waltz to the tune of your slow sadness.

trans: Gerald Moore & Ulli Beier

PATRICE EMERY LUMUMBA (1926–61), the first Premier of
the Republic of the Congo, was assassinated by his polititcal op-
ponents. In death he gained immortality throughout the African
continent as a symbol of Pan-Africanism. His one book, *Congo,
My Country,* was published posthumously.

DAWN IN THE HEART OF AFRICA

For a thousand years, you, African, suffered like a beast,
Your ashes strewn to the wind that roams the desert.
Your tyrants built the lustrous, magic temples
To preserve your soul, preserve your suffering.
Barbaric right of fist and the white right to a whip,
You had the right to die, you also could weep.
On your totem they carved endless hunger, endless bonds,
And even in the cover of the woods a ghastly cruel death
Was watching, snaky, crawling to you

Like branches from the holes and heads of trees
Embraced your body and your ailing soul.
Then they put a treacherous big viper on your chest:
On your neck they laid the yoke of fire-water,
They took your sweet wife for glitter of cheap pearls,
Your incredible riches that nobody could measure.
From your hut, the tom-toms sounded into dark of night
Carrying cruel laments up mighty black rivers
About abused girls, streams of tears and blood,
About ships that sailed to countries where the little man
Wallows in an anthill and where the dollar is king,
To that damned land which they called a motherland.
There your child, your wife were ground, day and night
In a frightful, merciless mill, crushing them in dreadful pain.
You are a man like others. They preach you to believe
That good white God will reconcile all men at last.
By fire you grieved and sang the moaning songs
Of a homeless beggar that sinks at strangers' doors.
And when a craze possessed you
And your blood boiled through the night
You danced, you moaned, obsessed by father's passion.

Like fury of a storm to lyrics of a manly tune
From a thousand years of misery a strength burst out of you
In metallic voice of jazz, in uncovered outcry
That thunders through the continent like gigantic surf.
The whole world surprised, wakes up in panic
To the violent rhythm of blood, to the violent rhythm of jazz,
The white man turning pallid over this new song
That carries torch of purple through the dark of night.

The dawn is here, my brother! Dawn! Look in our faces,
A new morning breaks in our old Africa.
Ours alone will now be the land, the water, mighty rivers
Poor African surrendered for a thousand years.
Hard torches of the sun will shine for us again

They'll dry the tears in eyes and spittle on your face.
The moment when you break the chains, the heavy fetters,
The evil, cruel times will go never to come again.
A free and gallant Congo will arise from black soil,
A free and gallant Congo—black blossom from black seed!

Madagascar

JEAN-JOSEPH REBÉARIVELO (1901–37), born at Antananarivo, Madagascar, of a noble but poor family, founded a literary review and led the way in the creation of a new Madagascan literature written in French. He became a drug addict and killed himself in a mood of despair brought on because the local officials would not let him visit France. Among his published poems are *La Coupe de cendres* (1924), *Sylves* (1927), *Volumes* (1928), *Vientes de la Mañana, Presque-songes* (1934), and an English translation entitled *24 Poems* (1963).

WHAT INVISIBLE RAT

What invisible rat,
Comes out of the walls of the night
Gnaws the milk-cake of the moon?
In the morning
He will be gone
Leaving bloodstained marks of teeth.

In the morning,
Those who have been drunk all night
And those who have just left the gaming tables
Seeing the moon
Will mutter
"Whose is that sixpence
Rolling on the green table?"
"Ah!" will say one
"He had lost everything
So he killed himself!"

And they all will snigger
And stagger and fall.
The moon will be gone.
The rat will have dragged it into his hole.

trans: Alan Ryder

FLAVIEN RANAIVO, born in 1914 near Antananarivo in Madagascar, is the son of the Governor of Arivonimamo. He learned to read music long before he learned the alphabet, so his poetic style is much influenced by song and ballad forms. Among his published volumes of verse are *L'Ombre et le vent* (1947) and *Mes chansons de toujours* (1955).

SONG OF A COMMON LOVER

Don't love me, my sweet,
like your shadow
for shadows fade at evening
and I want to keep you
right up to cockcrow;
nor like pepper
which makes the belly hot
for then I couldn't take you
when I'm hungry;
nor like a pillow
for we'd be together in the hours of sleep
but scarcely meet by day;
nor like rice
for once swallowed you think no more of it;
nor like soft speeches
for they quickly vanish;
nor like honey,
sweet indeed but too common.

Love me like a beautiful dream,
your life in the night,
my hope in the day;
like a piece of money,
ever with me on earth,
and for the great journey
a faithful comrade;
like a calabash,
intact, for drawing water;
in pieces, bridges for my guitar.

trans: Alan Ryder

Nigeria

HUNGER

(Oral Traditional)

Hunger makes a person climb up to the ceiling
And hold on to the rafters.
It makes a person lie down—
But not feel at rest.
It makes a person lie down—
Unable to stand.
It makes a person lie down—
And count the rafters.
When the Moslem is not hungry, he says:
"We are forbidden to eat monkey."
When Ibrahim is hungry he eats a baboon!
When hunger beats the woman in the harem,
She will run out into the street in daytime.
One who is hungry does not care for taboos.
One who is hungry does not care for death.
One who is hungry will take
Out of the sacrifice money.
When death shuts the door,
Hunger will open it.
"I have filled my belly yesterday"
Does not concern hunger.
There is no God like one's throat.
We have to sacrifice daily to it.

trans: Ulli Beier

GABRIEL OKARA, born in 1921 in the Ijaw country of the Niger Delta (Biafra), is considered by many to be the leading Nigerian poet. He has worked as a principal information officer in the Eastern Nigerian Government Service. He is deeply concerned with the problem of the development of a style in English capable of fully expressing the African view of life. His poems have appeared in many journals and his novel *The Voice* was published in 1964.

THE MYSTIC DRUM

The mystic drum beat in my inside
and fishes danced in the rivers
and men and women danced on land
to the rhythm of my drum

But standing behind a tree
with leaves around her waist
she only smiled with a shake of her head.

Still my drum continued to beat,
rippling the air with quickened
tempo compelling the quick
and the dead to dance and sing
with their shadows—

But standing behind a tree
with leaves around her waist
she only smiled with a shake of her head.

Then the drum beat with the rhythm
of the things of the ground
and invoked the eye of the sky
the sun and the moon and the river gods—
and the trees began to dance,
the fishes turned men
and men turned fishes
and things stopped to grow—

But standing behind a tree
with leaves around her waist
she only smiled with a shake of her head.

And then the mystic drum
in my inside stopped to beat—
and men became men,
fishes became fishes
and trees, the sun and the moon
found their places, and the dead
went to the ground and things began to grow.

And behind the tree she stood
with roots sprouting from her
feet and leaves growing on her head
and smoke issuing from her nose
and her lips parted in her smile
turned cavity belching darkness.

Then, then I packed my mystic drum
and turned away; never to beat so loud any more.

PIANO AND DRUMS

When at break of day at a riverside
I hear jungle drums telegraphing
the mystic rhythm, urgent, raw
like bleeding flesh, speaking of
primal youth and the beginning,
I see the panther ready to pounce,
the leopard snarling about to leap
and the hunters crouch with spears poised;

And my blood ripples, turns torrent,
topples the years and at once I'm
in my mother's lap a suckling;
at once I'm walking simple

paths with no innovations,
rugged, fashioned with the naked
warmth of hurrying feet and groping hearts
in green leaves and wild flowers pulsing.

Then I hear a wailing piano
solo speaking of complex ways
in tear-furrowed concerto;
of far-away lands
and new horizons with
coaxing diminuendo, counterpoint,
crescendo. But lost in the labyrinth
of its complexities, it ends in the middle
of a phrase at a dagger point.

And I lost in the morning mist
of an age at a riverside keep
wandering in the mystic rhythm
of jungle drums and the concerto.

AIG HIGO was born around 1929 in Nigeria, where he works
as a publisher's representative. He read English at Ibadan University and did postgraduate work at Leeds. His poetry has appeared in such anthologies as *Modern Poetry from Africa.*

HIDESONG

I struck tomorrow square in the face
Yesterday groaned and said,
"Please mind your steps today."
I left them swimming with today.

Hidesong
Birdsong
Unto my soul

> What funeral pyre rejects your bones?
> My spider soul is spinning
> Spinning
>   Spinning endlessly.

Scarabwise I tow my days along
Alone I tow my death along.

CHRISTOPHER OKIGBO (1932–67), born in the Ibo country of Eastern Nigeria, was killed in action with the Biafran Army. He has two published volumes of poetry entitled *Heavensgate* (1962) and *Limits* (1964) and his work appears in anthologies.

a poem from D I S T A N C E S

Death lay in ambush,
that evening in that island;
and the voice sought its echo,
that evening in that island,
and the eye lost its light,
and the light lost its shadow.

And the wind, eternal suitor of dead leaves,
unrolled his bandages to the finest swimmer . . .

And it was an evening without flesh of skeleton;
an evening with no silver bells to its tale;
without lanterns; without buntings;
and it was an evening without age or memory—

for we are talking of such commonplace things,
and on the brink of such great events—
and in the freezing tuberoses of the white
chamber, eyes that had lost their animal
colour—havoc of incandescent rays—
pinned me, cold to the marble stretcher,
           until my eyes lost their blood,
           and the blood lost its odour;

and the everlasting fire from the oblong window
forgot the taste of ash in the air's marrow . . .

Anguish and solitude . . .
Smothered, my scattered
cry, the dancers,
lost among their own
snares; the faces,
the hands, held captive;
the interspaces
reddening with blood . . .

And behind them all,
in smock of white cotton,
Death herself,
the chief celebrant,
in a cloud of incense,
paring her fingernails . . .

At her feet roll their heads like cut fruits;
about her fall
their severed members, numerous as locusts.
Like split wood left to dry,
the dismembered joints
of the ministrants pile high.

She bathes her knees in the blood of attendants,
her smock in the entrails of the ministrants . . .

WOLE SOYINKA, born in 1934 at Abeokuta, Nigeria, is an
actor, musician, producer, playwright, and poet. He has done
much to stimulate interest in theatrical life in Nigeria. His plays
have won prizes and been widely performed in Africa, Europe,
and America. In 1967 he was arrested by the Federal Government
for his political beliefs. His poetry appears in such anthologies as

Black Orpheus (of which he is an editor), and his other publications include *Five Plays* (1964) and a novel, *The Interpreters,* (1965).

TELEPHONE CONVERSATION

The price seemed reasonable, location
Indifferent. The landlady swore she lived
Off premises. Nothing remained
But self-confession. "Madam," I warned,
"I hate a wasted journey—I am African."
Silence. Silenced transmission of
Pressurized good-breeding. Voice, when it came,
Lipstick coated, long gold-rolled
Cigarette-holder pipped. Caught I was, foully.
"HOW DARK?" . . . I had not misheard . . . "ARE YOU
                                               LIGHT
OR VERY DARK?" Button B. Button A. Stench
Of rancid breath of public hide-and-speak.
Red booth. Red pillar-box. Red double-tiered
Omnibus squelching tar. It *was* real! Shamed
By ill-mannered silence, surrender
Pushed dumbfoundment of beg simplification.
Considerate she was, varying the emphasis—
"ARE YOU DARK? OR VERY LIGHT?" Revelation came.
"You mean—like plain or milk chocolate?"
Her assent was clinical, crushing in its light
Impersonality. Rapidly, wave-length adjusted,
I chose. "West African sepia"—and as afterthought,
"Down in my passport." Silence or spectroscopic
Flight of fancy, till truthfulness clanged her accent
Hard of the mouthpiece. "WHAT'S THAT?" conceding
"DON'T KNOW WHAT THAT IS." "Like brunette."
"THAT'S DARK, ISN'T IT?" "Not altogether.
Facially, I am brunette, but madam, you should see
The rest of me. Palm of my hand, soles of my feet

Are a peroxide blonde. Friction, caused—
Foolishly, madam—by sitting down, has turned
My bottom raven black— One moment madam!"—sensing
Her receiver rearing on the thunderclap
About my ears—"Madam," I pleaded, "wouldn't you rather
See for yourself?"

MICHAEL ECHERUO, born in 1937 in the Ibo country of Eastern Nigeria, is lecturer in English at the University of Nsukka.
His poems were first published in *Black Orpheus.*

MELTING POT

It is dark, now, and grave

This bowl of a world
That rings me round and round
And will not let me marvel enough
At this dull sky
At the ignorance of these men
Who cannot know what chance can do

I shudder
Before this bowl of a world,
At this dull sky.

Will they not, all of them,
Call me names when they hear
Their blind man of this city
Stumbled on an udara underfoot
And lost it in the search for more?

Wish they could see half
What my eyes see, or know
Half what I know!
The Century's blind man!

Ghana

AQUAH LALUAH (Gladys May Casely-Hayford) (1904–50), born of a distinguished Fanti family at Axim on the Gold Coast, taught school in Freetown, Sierra Leone. She was educated in England and Wales. Her early poems were published in *The Atlantic Monthly* and in a small volume entitled *Take 'Um So.*

NATIVITY

Within a native hut, ere stirred the dawn,
Unto the Pure One was an Infant born,
Wrapped in blue lappah that His mother dyed,
Laid on His father's home-tanned deerskin hide,
The Babe still slept, by all things glorified.
Spirits of black bards burst their bonds and sang
"Peace upon earth" until the heavens rang.
All the black babies who from earth had fled
Peeped through the clouds—then gathered round His head,
Telling of things a baby needs to do,
When first he opes his eyes on wonder new;
Telling Him that sleep was sweetest rest,
All comfort came from His black mother's breast.
Their gift was Love, caught from the springing sod,
Whilst tears and laughter were the gifts of God.
Then all the Wise Men of the past stood forth,
Filling the air, East, West, and South and North,
And told Him of the joy that wisdom brings
To mortals in their earthly wanderings.

[164

The children of the past shook down each bough,
Wreathed franipani blossoms for His brow,
They put pink lilies in His mother's hand,
And heaped for both the first fruits of the land.
His father cut some palm fronds, that the air
Be coaxed to zephyrs while He rested there.
Birds trilled their hallelujahs; all the dew
Trembled with laughter, till the Babe laughed too.
Black women brought their love so wise,
And kissed their motherhood into His mother's eyes.

GEORGE AWOONOR-WILLIAMS, born in 1935 at Wheta in
the Togo Region of Ghana, is of Sierra Leonian and Togolese
descent. He was educated at Achimota and the University of
Ghana. He has worked for the Ghana Film Industry Corporation,
in the Institute of African Stuides, and is editor of the literary review *Okyeame*. His first volume of poems is entitled *Rediscovery* (1964).

REDISCOVERY

When our tears are dry on the shore
and the fishermen carry their nets home
and the seagulls return to bird island
and the laughter of the children recedes at night,
there shall still linger the communion we forged,
the feast of oneness whose ritual we partook of.
There shall still be the eternal gateman
who will close the cemetery doors
and send the late mourners away.
It cannot be the music we heard that night
that still lingers in the chambers of memory.
It is the new chorus of our forgotten comrades
and the halleluyahs of our second selves.

KWESI BREW, born in 1938 at Cape Coast in Ghana, first published his poetry in the Ghanaian literary review *Okyeame*. His work appears in every major anthology of African verse.

THE LONELY TRAVELLER

Leave him alone, sweet enemy,
For the mothers of the earth
Have sanctioned his freedom;
And in priceless peace
He floats in ethereal bliss,
A traveller on the shores of eternity.
You saw the genial mists of courage:
With his faith as his spear
And his past as his shield,
He battled the bondage of bludgeons
Now far on the horizon
The red suns set,
The tired suns set
To turn old nights into new dawns,
And people the skies with black stars.
And our hands that slept on the drums
Have found their cunning
To cheer the lonely traveller
Meandering his weary way
On the green and golden hills of Africa.

A. L. MILNER-BROWN is a native of Ghana where he is now active as teacher, newspaperman, and free-lance writer. His poetry appears in *Poems from Black Africa* and other anthologies.

WHO KNOWS?

Who knows? This Africa so richly blest
With golden lands and fronded palms in air,
The envy of great nations far and near,
May yet the world lead back to peace and rest,
Goodwill to all. Who knows? Who knows?

And when the fullness of God's time has come
And men of diverse colors, tribes and castes
Have owned Him King; when hate and sin are passed,
The Prince of Peace may found His home
In Africa at last. Who knows? Who knows?

Liberia

ROLAND TOMBEKAI DEMPSTER is one of the founders of the Society of Liberian Authors in Monrovia. He was educated at Liberia College and later studied journalism in the United States. Now editor-in-chief of *The Liberian Age,* he has published books of poetry and prose.

AFRICA'S PLEA

I am not you—
but you will not
give me a chance,
will not let me be *me*.

"If I were you"—
but you know
I am not you,
yet you will not
let me be *me*.

You meddle, interfere
in my affairs
as if they were yours
and you were me.

You are unfair, unwise,
foolish to think
that I can be you,

talk, act
and think like you.

God made me *me*.
He made you *you*.
For God's sake
Let me be *me*.

Gambia

LENRIE PETERS, born in 1932 in Bathurst, Gambia, was educated at Bathurst, Freetown, and Cambridge University where he obtained his medical degree. Although he practices as a surgeon, he also sings, broadcasts, and writes. He has published two volumes of poetry including *Satellites* (1967) and a novel, *The Second Round* (1964).

AFTER THEY PUT DOWN THEIR OVERALLS

After they put down their overalls
And turn off the lathes
They do not return to the women
After they have bathed
Instead, with Hyena's thirst
They turn to the open-air bar
To swallow the hook of imported liquor
As they sit reckless across the log
Hypnotized by the bees.

They belch the arrogance of doubt
As they lie in refined stupor
Waiting for the sharp sun
To show them the way out.
Less sure than when they took the potion
They lumber back to the clever tools
They do not love and do not understand
Hoping the sun's anger would cool
So they can carry their dark glasses in their hand.

Kenya

JOSEPH E. KARIUKI was born in 1931 at Banana Hill, Kenya. He holds a degree from Cambridge University, has had his verse broadcast from the Overseas Service of the British Broadcasting Corporation, and his work appears in several anthologies.

NEW LIFE

It will rain tonight,
I smell it in the air,
And how we have waited.

My love said she would come with the rain.

A gentle knock at the door—
Palpable thudding in my breast.

A gust of wind blows out the tiny candle,
A momentary torrential outburst,
Then a flash that lights up
Scorching eyes.
A crack to end the world:
An unbearable brief eternity of silence
And then the rain.

It comes heaving, tearing, bearing down,
Surging in impatient billows to drain its source,
Till unable to bear its own forces
It settles to a timeless steady flow
Endless.

There is calm in the air,
And greater calm by my side.

Tomorrow the village women go planting
Their seed in the hungry ground:
And life is born anew.

South Africa

DAVID GRANMER T. BERENG, Southern Sotho antiquarian and poet, is an authority on traditional literature of Lesotho. He has published *Lithothokiso tsa Moshoeshoe le tse ling* (1931), a collection of eleven long poems in praise of Moshesh the great Sotho general who led his people in their struggles with the invading British.

THE BIRTH OF MOSHESH

What began that bustle in the village,
Why all the stirring in the yards?
What moves the restless women from hut to hut
Or has the young men glancing round?
What sets menfolk at each other's ears,
Of what dread things do the drums speak;
What starts the hollow bull-horns booming,
Strums on the sounding calabash strings
And what reed notes these on the shrill pipes?
See now the smiling women's faces,
All the young men amazed,
And the elders speaking in tough riddles.

Bright and clear the veld,
Echoes ringing in the hills,
And the sound hung above the peaks
And all the cliff caves rebounding.
The wild beasts roamed uneasily
And the antelopes went skipping away;

The animals went unheeded in this daze of news
And men and women left wondering:

To Libenyane a man-child is born.
He emerged with a shield gripped in his hand.
In his face the people read great deeds
Heralded before they came to be;
And things were dark to ponder.
For men saw plants grow as they watched
And flowers bloom luxuriant,
Stars streamed in the day sky
Like midnight lightnings.
They saw flame-tongues in the sun
And in their huts men laid aside their blankets.
The moon stood still against the sky
Like a shy bride before her husband's father.
Through a cranny the whispering was heard,
The cattle also seemed to listen
And soon their lowing was loud;
The wet-nosed household gods bellowing out,
Lions roaring in the plains
Roar and give way before the King.
Leopards roaring in the krantzes
Roar and give way before the King.
The wild beasts made the world tremble
For him, Moshesh, though but an infant,
Man-child suckled on the milk of antelopes.

Thus and thus we knew Thesele was born
For when born, he Letlama, son of Mokhachane,
When he was born the tribes were glad.
The day the great Lepoqo saw the light
We sang new songs unknown to us
And for us the young girls swung in dance.
Then it was we could say:
Halala! You Zulus of Natal!
We too have a true chief today.

SAM DUBY R. SUTU, who died in 1965, was educated at Pius XII College in Roma, Lesotho. He was principal of the Moshoe-shoe Secondary School at Matatiele in the Transkei. Among his publications is a play, *Ho tla na Lebenya Paballong* (1962) and a volume of poems, *Mathe a Ntsi* (1963).

NIGHT

Night, and on all sides only the folding quiet,
In the sky the wide staring eyes of the stars:
Looking from them maybe the earth shines too
As winking softly, they watch in their delight
This loveliness that lies asleep in all its peace.

And everywhere around, and coming in on me
Is a great stillness, unutterable silence in the open,
And not a grass-blade nor a single reed that trembles,
No sound rises anywhere, no murmur, nothing;
Night, and on all sides only the folding quiet.

A stirring of the air, a little thing, brushes my cheek,
A faint wind, spirit of life in this night.
The flowers, the wild creatures, all things made on earth
Now are blanketed in quietness and still
As if their hearts were giving thanks to their Creator.

Were I not apart in my own loneliness here
I would say: "My brother, turn around and look
Far off towards the east along the mountains, gaze
Above the eastern peaks, ours for a little while,
And see what fills my eyes—the golden light!"

.   .   .   .

I would say: "Brother, stand here by my side tonight,
Share this with me, this earth, this sky."
The moon, gold-skinned ruler of the night, shows her rim—

First a narrow husk, and then—the great round gourd!
And I long to say: "What lovelier than this!"

You would feel then as I feel, my brother,
Like small children struck by some thing of wonder,
Their faces rapt with smiles and eyes alight
Their small breasts rise and fall, hearts beat—
Then you and I would stamp our feet in joy.

Yet here as I stand single in my loneliness
I cannot shout against the silence of the night.
No sign or sound comes of the laughing-dove
And the owl, familiar of witches, still keeps dumb.
Night, and on all sides only the folding quiet.

.   .   .   .

Night, and on all sides only the folding quiet,
In the sky the wide staring eyes of the stars:
Looking from them maybe the earth shines too.
My star, never hide from me but show my way
That I too may let my light shine through the dark.

B. W. VILAKAZI (1906–47), born at Groutville, Natal, was joint
compiler of the standard Zulu-English Dictionary. He was Lec-
turer in African Studies at Witwatersrand, where the Vilakazi
Award for Nguni Literature has been established in his memory.
He published two volumes of verse in Zulu entitled *Inkondlo ka-
Zulu* and *Amal ezulu*.

IN THE GOLD MINES

Rumble on, machines of the gold mines
Thundering from first light to sun's sinking:
Ah, stop plaguing me, I'll wake up.
Rumble on, machines, and drown out

The groans of the black working men
Whose bodies ache with throbbing weals,
Struck by the thuds of the stifling air,
On their limbs the stink of sweat and dirt:
Sapped of the vigor of their loins.

.   .   .   .

I've heard it said that down the pits
Are nations upon nations of the Blacks,
And men of these tribes raise the white dunes
That make the angry spirits wonder.
There's a story told about the mine machines
That when they shrieked a small black mouse
Peeped out stunned and in a daze;
It was trapped and turned into a mole,
Burrowed in the earth, and so was seen the gleam of gold.

Yes, these burrowers dug underground
And sent up the towering white dumps.
They rooted deep and the ground heaved higher,
Today outtopping the hill of Isandlwana;
I climb up sweeping the sweat out of my eyes,
And here at the crest I watch the dust-coils
Smoke-white that weave and shift
Below my feet, and under shaded eyes
I see how they blot out the world.

.   .   .   .

We yielded and came up from our thatched huts
And were herded here together like yoke-oxen;
We left our dark corn and curds and milk
To be fed instead an alien mess of porridge.
Our family pride is gone, we are children,
The world is clearly turned heels over head.
Wakened up at dawn, stood in a row!

Where have you known of a man once curried
Who sees with both eyes open and stands alive?

.   .   .   .

My brother will plod along carrying a pick
A shovel slung over one shoulder,
And his feet cased in iron-shod boots;
He too will go below following me,
The ground takes us burrowers at a gulp.
If I should die down in the deep levels
What matter? Just who am I anyway?
Day after day, you poor sufferer,
The men drop dead, they keel over while I watch.

Such towers were not here to scale
That time I first went underground,
Still I recall the raw deal that I got.
I thought, I'll pack my goods and get home,
But there—ruins and bare fields struck me.
I scratched my head, went into a hut
And asked: Where is my wife, her parents?
They said: The whiteman called them up to work.
Then I was dumb, my mouth sewn up in silence.

.   .   .   .

Not so loud there, you machines;
Though whitemen may be without pity
Must you too, made of iron, treat me thus?
Hold off your roaring now in those mines
And listen awhile to what we say to you
Just in case we may be unforgiving
On that fine day which is still to come
When we stand up and say: Things of iron
You are slaves to us, the children of the Blacks.

Be careful, though I go unarmed today

There was a time when from these worn-out arms
Long-bladed spears were flung far and wide
Whose whirling dimmed the whole earth;
They shook the empire of the She Elephant *
Thinned out Paul's ** boers—then I was struck down.
Now I am forever dreaming, child of iron,
That this earth of my forefathers once again
Will be restored to the rightful Black hands.

.   .   .   .

This your fatherland today and yesterday
Is pillaged by the foreign conquerors
Grown rich out of the spoil of nation on nation,
Yet I and this whole line of ours
Who are black are left with nothing of nothing.
We come to the surface and we see the grass
Green to the furthermost rim of sky,
We gaze all about us and call out loud
Wo! But again you do not reply.

Thunder on, engines of the gold mines,
My hands may tremble with the pain,
My feet swell in my boots and stab me,
I have no salve to soothe them for
The whitemen sell their drugs for cash.
Roar on, only stop jarring on my ears,
I have served the white employers well
And now my soul weighs heavily in me.
Run slow, let sleep come to me entranced,
Deep sleep that seals up my eyes
Thinking no longer of tomorrow and the dawn.
Come, release me sleep, to rise far off
Far in the ancient birthplace of my race:

* Queen Victoria
** President Kruger

Sleep and dreams from which there is no waking,
Clasped in my vanished people's arms
Under the green hills of the sky.

RICHARD RIVE, born in 1931 in Cape Town, South Africa,
is the son of an American Negro seaman and a Cape Coloured
woman. His short stories have appeared in German and Scandi-
navian countries and his poems have been included in such anthologies as *Poems from Black Africa*.

WHERE THE RAINBOW ENDS

Where the rainbow ends
There's going to be a place, brother,
Where the world can sing all sorts of songs,
And we're going to sing together, brother,
You and I, though you're white and I'm not.
It's going to be a sad song, brother,
Because we don't know the tune,
And it's a difficult tune to learn.
But we can learn, brother, you and I.
There's no such tune as a black tune.
There's no such tune as a white tune.
There's only music, brother,
And it's music we're going to sing
Where the rainbow ends.

Angola

ANTONIO JACINTO, born in Luanda, Angola, is included in Andrade's *Caderno* and *Modern Poetry from Africa*.

MONANGAMBA

On that big estate there is no rain
it's the sweat of my brow that waters the crops:

On that big estate there is coffee ripe
and that cherry-redness
is drops of my blood turned sap.

> The coffee will be roasted,
> ground, and crushed,
> will turn black, black with the colour of the
> > *contratado.*

Black with the colour of the *contratado!*

Ask the birds that sing,
the streams in carefree wandering
and the high wind from inland:

> Who gets up early? Who goes to toil?
> Who is it carries on the long road
> the hammock or bunch of kernels?
> Who reaps and for pay gets scorn
> rotten maize, rotten fish,
> ragged clothes, fifty *angolares*
> beating for biting back?

Who?

> Who makes the millet grow
> and the orange groves to flower?
> —Who?

Who gives the money for the boss to buy
cars, machinery, women
    and Negro heads for the motors?

Who makes the white man prosper,
grow big-bellied—get much money?
—Who?

And the birds that sing,
the streams in carefree wandering
and the high wind from inland
will answer:

> —Monangambeeee . . . .

Ah! Let me at least climb the palm trees
Let me drink wine, palm wine
and fuddled by my drunkness forget

> —Monangambeeee . . . .

trans: Alan Ryder

NOTE: *Contratado*—contract labourer
       Angolares—unit of money

São Tomé

ALDO DO ESPIRITO SANTO, born in 1906 in São Tomé, works as a teacher as well as a poet. His work appears in literary reviews of São Tomé, in *Caderno* (Andrade), and *Modern Poetry from Africa.*

WHERE ARE THE MEN SEIZED IN THIS WIND OF MADNESS?

Blood falling in drops to the earth
men dying in the forest
and blood falling, falling . . .
on those cast into the sea . . .
Fernao Dias for ever in the story
of Ilha Verde, red with blood,
of men struck down
in the vast arena of the quay.
Alas the quay, the blood, the men,
the fetters, the lash of beatings
resound, resound, resound
dropping in the silence of prostrated lives
of cries, and howls of pain
from men who are men no more,
in the hands of nameless butchers.
Ze Mulato, in the story of the quay
shooting men in the silence
of bodies falling.
Alas Ze Mulato, Ze Mulato,

The victims cry for vengeance
The sea, the sea of Fernao Dias
devouring human lives
is bloody red.
—We are risen—
Our eyes are turned to you.
Our lives entombed
in fields of death,
men of the Fifth of February
men fallen in the furnace of death
imploring pity
screaming for life,
dead without air, without water
they all arise
from the common grave
and upright in the chorus of justice
cry for vengeance . . .
The fallen bodies in the forest,
the homes, the homes of men
destroyed in the gulf
of ravening fire,
lives incinerated,
raise the unaccustomed chorus of justice
crying for vengeance.
And all you hangmen
all you torturers
sitting in the dock:
—What have you done with my people? . . .
—What do you answer?
—Where is my people? . . .
And I answer in the silence
of voices raised
demanding justice . . .
One by one, through all the line . . .
For you, tormentors,

forgiveness has no name.
Justice shall be heard.
And the blood of lives fallen
in the forests of death,
innocent blood
drenching the earth
in a silence of terrors
shall make the earth fruitful,
crying for justice.
It is the flame of humanity
singing of hope
in a world without bonds
where liberty
is the fatherland of men ...

trans: Alan Ryder

Mozambique

JOSÉ CRAVEIRINHA was born in 1922 at Lourenço Marques, Mozambique, where he has worked as a journalist. His poems have appeared in such anthologies as *African Writing Today*.

POEM OF THE FUTURE CITIZEN

I came from somewhere
from a Nation which does not yet exist.
I came and I am here!

Not I alone was born
nor you nor any other . . .
but brothers.

I have love to give in handfuls.
Love of what I am
and nothing more.

I have a heart
and cries which are not mine alone.

I come from a country which does not yet exist.

Ah! I have love in plenty to give
of what I am.
I!
A man among many
citizen of a Nation which has yet to exist.

trans: Dorothy Guedes & Philippa Rumsey

RUI NOGAR. A pseudonym for a writer who wishes to remain anonymous.

POEM OF THE CONSCRIPTED WARRIOR

He went there
Afraid
Of being afraid.

(Oh Our Lady of Anything
In my village
I left my wife behind.)

He went there
With the shame
Of feeling ashamed.

(Perhaps I might even kill children;
I have two children, oh Lord . . .)

He went there
Involuntarily
He went there
And the courage was not his own
And the hate was not his own
Not his own
Not at all
But he went
Infected with blood lust
He killed killed killed
Until one day
Oh! irony
On that day
There was sun
There was hope
There was his wife

There were his children his mother a letter

There was so much
But all crumbled away
All
In the treacherous cackling
Of the grenades
With yellow beaks
And red tails ...

trans: Dorothy Guedes & Philippa Rumsey

NOEMIA DE SOUSA, born in 1927 at Lourenço Marques, is the first African woman to achieve a genuine reputation as a modern poet. Her poetry appears in many Brazilian, Angolan, and Mozambique journals.

APPEAL

Who has strangled the tired voice
of my forest sister?
On a sudden, her call to action
was lost in the endless flow of night and day.
No more it reaches me every morning,
wearied with long journeying,
mile after mile drowned
in the everlasting cry: Macala!

No, it comes no more, still damp with dew,
leased with children and submission ...
One child on her back, another in her womb
—always, always, always!
And a face all composed in a gentle look,
whenever I recall that look I feel
my flesh and blood swell tremulous,
throbbing to revelations and affinities ...

—But who has stopped her immeasurable look
from feeding my deep hunger after comradeship
that my poor table never will serve to satisfy?

Io mamane, who can have shot the noble voice
of my forest sister?
What mean and brutal rhino-whip
has lashed until it killed her?

—In my garden the seringa blooms.
But with an evil omen in its purple flower,
in its intense inhuman scent;
and the wrap of tenderness spread by the sun
over the light mat of petals
has waited since summer for my sister's child
to rest himself upon it . . .
In vain, in vain,
a chirico sings and sings perched among the garden reeds,
for the little boy of my missing sister,
the victim of the forest's vaporous dawns.
Ah, I know, I know: at the last there was a glitter
of farewell in those gentle eyes,
and her voice came like a murmur hoarse,
tragic and despairing . . .
O Africa, my motherland, answer me:
What was done to my forest sister,
that she comes no more to the city with her eternal little ones
(one on her back, one in her womb),
with her eternal charcoal-vendor's cry?
O Africa, my motherland,
you at least will not forsake my heroic sister,
she shall live in the proud memorial of yours arms!

trans: Dorothy Guedes & Philippa Rumsey

VALENTE GOENHA MALANGATANA was born in 1936 in
Marracuene, Mozambique, and is both a painter and a poet. His
poems have appeared in *Black Orpheus* as well as other anthologies.

WOMAN

In the cool waters of the river
we shall have fish that are huge
which shall give the sign of
the end of the world perhaps
because they will make an end of woman
woman who adorns the fields
woman who is the fruit of man.

The flying fish makes an end of searching
because woman is the gold of man
when she sings she ever seems
like the fado-singer's well-tuned guitar
when she dies, I shall cut off
her hair to deliver me from sin.

Woman's hair shall be the blanket
over my coffin when another Artist
calls me to Heaven to paint me
woman's breasts shall be my pillow
woman's eye shall open up for me the way to heaven
woman's belly shall give birth to me up there
and woman's glance shall watch me
as I go up to Heaven.

trans: Dorothy Guedes & Philippa Rumsey

U.S.A.

Until two world wars brought the United States into the financial and political leadership of the West, America suffered from a cultural inferiority complex. Its major writers disguised themselves as alcoholics, sailors, rural humorists, or simply emigrated to more congenial lands. The fact was that most Americans, until quite recently, suspected that musicians and painters and poets were cranks, reds, fagots, or simply phonies.

If there was little incentive for white Americans to write poetry, blacks had even less. Black slaves had been punished for their literacy by having their fingers chopped off. In Cuba, in 1820, the black poet, Juan Francisco Monzano, was discovered at the age of eleven to be composing and reciting poetry and for this "unnatural crime" was gagged and rudely tortured. Down South after the Civil War a black man who showed his education was being "uppity"—a social crime that called for summary retribution in the view of many Southern whites. Because most blacks and whites were ignorant of the eternal contribution of Africa to mankind's achievement, because most were unaware that black men in Latin America had become leading figures in politics and the arts, most Americans have, until very recently, felt somewhat uncom-

fortable about blacks being poets. This was a curious blind
spot, since black contributions to American folk and popular
song had been the chief glories of the national tradition.

British-American pioneers mainly expressed themselves as
ballad makers, hymn composers, and square dancers. Flex-
ibly, black Americans turned their hands to these new gênres.
The black peasants of the South rhymed up our favorite
American ballads—*Frankie, John Henry, Casey Jones*. They
transformed the sturdy, death-ridden and moralistic white
folk hymns into the spirituals, unmatched for simple gran-
deur and for poignant humanity. Through all this golden
stream of folklore there sounded the blue notes of irony and
sorrow, but a stronger current was an ancient African joy in
being alive and experiencing a real world—

> *My name is Ron, I works in the sand*
> *But I'd rather be a nigger than a poor white man.*
> *Me and my gal went walking down the road*
> *The wind from her feet knocking Sugar in the Gourd.**
> *Sugar in the gourd and the gourd on the ground*
> *If you want to get the sugar, you got to roll the gourd around.*

In the dance, for which stiff-waisted western Europeans
have never shown much talent, the blacks quickly showed
their mastery. Long before the Revolution no big plantation
ball was a success without its Negro banjo pickers and high-
steppers. The first American ballet, played in Philadelphia
before Thomas Jefferson and George Washington, was in
blackface—a testament to the excitement of Negro dancing. In
the minstrel show, the mainstay of America's entertainment in
the Nineteenth Century, white men masqueraded as blacks,
attempting to imitate their sliding, heel-free, hip-joggling
steps. Here blacks, for the first time, found some secure foot-
hold in the arts. James Bland, composer of *Golden Slippers*,
and John Work, author of *The Blue-Tail Fly*, were re-

* An old Southern banjo tune.

warded for writing poetry that might be fairly called Afro-
American . . .

> . . . *The pony run, he jump, he pitch,*
> *He threw my master in the ditch.*
> *He died, and the jury wondered why—*
> *The verdict was the blue-tail fly.*
> *They lay him under a 'simmon tree;*
> *His epitaph is there to see:*
> *"Beneath this stone I'm forced to lie,*
> *A victim of the blue-tail fly.*
> > *Jimmy crack corn, and I don't care,*
> > *My massa's gone away . . .*

While the big river of the blues was rising in the Mississippi delta to pour its dark poetry into the ear of the world,
the black piano wizards of Sedalia, Missouri, were composing
a lacey and syncopated style for the piano called "ragtime"
that was soon the rage of city folk. The gellid tinkle of ragtime became the background music for America's national
drama—the Western. When the black geniuses of the Mississippi Valley had mastered white Europe's most complex musical instrument, they turned their attention to orchestral
music and, in hot jazz, swing, and a score of other styles, soon
out-stripped their white teachers. Their "hot" music—one of
the first international musical languages—drew the attention
of the whole world to the American Negro.

The triumphal sound of jazz, floating through the salons
of New York's bohemia in the twenties, ushered in the Harlem Renaissance. It suddenly became fashionable to be black.
While white intellectuals were pretending to be oppressed
proletarians, lusting after life, the poets of Harlem were all
these things in fact. Giant and romantic figures stalked
through this "cultured hell"—James Weldon Johnson with
his epic sermons; W.E.B. Dubois, one of America's first and,
by all odds, her most courageous sociologist; Toomer, Cullen,
and MacKay, who matched in polish the best of white poets;

Langston Hughes and Sterling Brown, who built their poems
on the solid rock of black folklore and vernacular.

A current of interest was set free in these golden years of
Harlem that linked American blacks to the West Indies. The
Garvey movement was only one reflection of this turn toward
Africa. Soon, however, the depression involved the black
community in a common national disaster. The subsequent
optimism of the Roosevelt years, and the experience of integration and acceptance in the Federal Arts projects created
a temporarially sanguine mood. Most black writers joined
enthusiastically in the fight against race-prejudiced fascism
in World War II, marching in a newly integrated army and
taking hope from this change.

In the first political campaigns after the War all parties,
spurred on by Henry Wallace's call for immediate and total
integration, had to commit themselves against America's Jim
Crow system. Tens of thousands of disillusioned Negroes left
the South to change the racial balance in Northern communities and schools. Young people, black and white, sometimes
fought each other with knives and bicycle chains, yet learned
to know each other in the American cities of the fifties and
early sixties. A new hot music united white and black into a
rock generation that shocked their parents with the repeti-
tious African song style, with pelvis-twisting black dances, a
free and easy acceptance of sexual intercourse and interracial
dating. Soon these young people were sitting down together
in Southern cafés, marching together against Southern sheriffs, and going to jail together. Together they waded onto
segregated beaches and into the whole Southern segregated
system. In five years their unity cracked a solid South that
experts had predicted would take a hundred years to change.

This was a time of oratory and of marching songs, of moral
and political victories, and of dreams of an integrated and
just America. Today these dreams are only half realized. The
establishment is molasses-slow in enforcing the new, legally

enacted integration laws. The old system digs its heels in and refuses to change overnight. A new generation appears that has learned from the folk song revival and the integration movement—from Woodie Guthrie, Bobby Dylan, Muddy Waters, and Otis Redding—that everyone has his thing and can be a poet. While the white kids devote themselves to the mysteries of the blues, it can be said that everyone in the black community is either writing or reading poetry, poetry that straightforwardly demands a new world. The poets feel an identity with their forbears—African and slave. They are torn between the desire to write and the need to act. Writes Juan Hernandez Cruz, a young Puerto Rican,

> *when poems start to*
> *knock down walls to*
> *choke politicians*
> *when poems scream &*
> *begin to break the air*
>
> *that is the time of*
> *true poets that is*
> *the time of greatness*
>
> *a true poet aiming*
> *poems & watching things*
> *fall to the ground*
> *it is a great day.*

Oral Traditionals

I VISION GOD

(A Folk-Sermon)

I vision God standing
on the heights of Heaven,
Throwing the devil like
A burning torch
Over the gulf
Into the valleys of hell.
His eye the lightning's flash,
His voice the thunder's roll.
Wid one hand He snatched
The sun from its socket,
And the other He clapped across the moon.

I vision God wringing
A storm from the heavens;
Rocking the world
Like an earthquake;
Blazing the sea
Wid a trail er fire.
His eye the lightning's flash,
His voice the thunder's roll.
Wid one hand He snatched
The sun from its socket,
And the other He clapped across the moon.

I vision God standing
On a mountain

Of burnished gold,
Blowing His breath
Of silver clouds
Over the world.
His eye the lightning's flash,
His voice the thunder's roll.
Wid one hand He snatched
The sun from its socket,
And the other He clapped across the moon.

from *Jonah's Gourd Vine* by Z. N. Hurston

DIVES AND LAZ'US*

Wo, his purple an' linen, too,
  Ring dat big bell;
Don't keer what sort-a rags fer you,
  Ring dat big bell;
Dine sumptious ev'y day,
  Ring dat big bell;
Tell Laz'us go away.

  Ring-a dat big bell,
  Dat bigges' big one!
  Tell-a me whut he done done
  Way down in hell!

Laz'us lay outside,
  Ring-a dat big bell;
Dogs lick his so' side,
  Ring-a dat big bell;
But when he bof die,
  Ring-a dat big bell,
Laz'us he even up-high.

Rich man I hears folks tell,
  Ring-a dat big bell,

* An ante-bellum spiritual discovered by John Lomax.

Dropped into lownes' hell,
  Ring-a dat big bell;
Laz'us lay close an' fast,
  Ring-a dat big bell,
In Ab'ham's breas' at last.

     from *American Ballads and Folk Songs*

LOVE

Love is a funny thing
Shaped like a lizard,
Run down your heart strings
And tickle your gizzard.

You can fall from a mountain,
You can fall from above,
But the great fall is
When you fall in love.

PRECIOUS THINGS

Hold my rooster, hold my hen,
Pray don't touch my Grecian Bend.

Hold my bonnet, hold my shawl,
Pray don't touch my waterfall.

Hold my hands by the finger tips,
But pray don't touch my sweet little lips.

OLD MARSE JOHN *

Old Marse John came ridin' by,
  "Say, Marse John, that mule's gonna die."
  "If he do, I'll tan his skin,
   And if he don't, I'll ride him agin."

 * A folksong from the days of slavery composed in the blackfaced minstrel
vein.

CHORUS:
O mourner, you shall be free,
Yes, mourner, you shall be free,
When the good Lord sets you free.

My old mistis promise me,
When she died she'd set me free,
She lived so long, she got so po',
She left old Sambo pullin' at his hoe.

My old mistis lyin' in the leaves,
Head full of lice, stockin' full of fleas,
There was old mistis dead and gone,
But here was old Sambo a-hoein' the corn.

My gal Sal, she sho is a card,
She works right out in the white folks' yard,
Cooks the goose, gives me the stuffin',
She thinks I'm workin', I ain't doin' nothin'.

She kills the turkey, saves me the bone,
Drinks the beer, saves me the foam,
She kills the chicken, saves me the wing,
Thinks I'm workin', ain't doin' a thing.

I likes my wife, I likes my baby,
I likes my flapjacks floatin' in gravy,
I likes my coffee, I likes it strong,
When I get to eatin', just bring the butter 'long.

Some folks say that a preacher won't steal,
I caught two in my cornfield,
Preachin' and prayin' all the time,
And pullin' my melons off the vine.

from *Folk Music of North America*

GO DOWN, OLD HANNAH*

Go down, old Hannah,
Doncha rise no mo',
If you rise in the mornin',
Bring Judgement Day.

You ought come on this Brazos,
Nineteen and four,
You could find a dead man
On every turn row.

You ought come on this Brazos,
Nineteen and ten,
They was drivin' the women
Like they do the men.

Moon in the mornin',
'Fore the sun does rise,
Well, I thought about my woman,
Hang my head an' cry.

Well, the sun was shin',
An' the men was flyin',
Ol' Captain was hollerin',
We was almost dyin'.

Well, I looked at old Hannah,
She was turnin' red,
And I looked at my partner,
He was almost dead.

One of these mornin's,
An' it won't be long,
That man's gonna call me,
An' I'll be gone.

* A work song from the Texas prison farms for blacks that pleads with
Old Hannah, the sun, to go down and cease to torment the worker in the
cane fields.

So go down, old Hannah,
Doncha rise no mo',
If you rise in the mornin',
Set the world on fire.

from American Ballads and Folk Songs

STAGOLEE*

It was early, early one mornin',
When I heard my bulldog bark,
Stagolee and Billy Lyons
Was squabblin' in the dark.

Stagolee told Billy Lyons,
"What do you think of that?
You win all my money, Billy,
Now you spit in my Stetson hat."

Stagolee, he went a-walkin'
In the red-hot, broilin' sun—
Says, "Bring me my six-shooter,
Lawd, I wants my forty-one."

Stagolee, he went a-walkin'
Through the mud and through the sand.
Says, "I feel mistreated this mornin',
I could kill most any man."

Billy Lyons told Stagolee,
"Please don't take my life,
I've got three little helpless chillun
And one poor, pitiful wife."

"Don't care nothin' about your chillun,
And nothin' about your wife,
You done mistreated me, Billy,
And I'm bound to take your life."

* Ballad of the Memphis rounder who was so mean that he took over hell
from the devil.

He shot him three times in the shoulder,
Lawd, and three times in the side,
Well, the last time he shot him
Cause Billy Lyons to die.

Stagolee told Mrs Billy,
"You don't believe yo' man is dead;
Come into the bar-room,
See the hole I shot in his head."

The high sheriff told the deputies,
"Get your pistols and come with me.
We got to go 'rest that
Bad man Stagolee."

The deputies took their pistols
And they laid them on the shelf—
"If you want that bad man Stagolee,
Go 'rest him by yourself."

High sheriff ask the bartender,
"Who can that bad man be?"
"Speak softly," said the bartender,
"It's that bad man Stagolee."

He touch Stack on the shoulder,
Say, "Stack, why don't you run?"
"I don't run, white folks,
When I got my forty-one."

The hangman put the mask on,
Tied his hands behind his back,
Sprung the trap on Stagolee
But his neck refuse to crack.

Hangman, he got frightened,
Said, "Chief, you see how it be—
I can't hang this man,
Better set him free."

Three hundred dollar funeral,
Thousand dollar hearse,
Satisfaction undertaker
Put Stack six feet in the earth.

Stagolee, he told the Devil,
Says, "Come on and have some fun—
You stick me with your pitchfork,
I'll shoot you with my forty-one."

Stagolee took the pitchfork,
And he laid it on the shelf.
Says, "Stand back, Tom Devil,
I'm gonna rule Hell by myself."

Bama's version from *American Folk Songs*

I GOT THE BLUES

I woke up this mornin' with the blues all round my bed,
Yes, I woke up this morning with the blues all round my bed,
Went to eat my breadfast, had the blues all in my bread.

"Good mornin', blues, blues, how do you do?"
"I'm feelin' pretty well, but, pardner, how are you?"

Yes, I woke up this morning, 'bout an hour 'fore day,
Reached and grabbed the pillow where my baby used to lay.

If you ever been down, you know just how I feel,
Feel like an engine, ain't got no drivin' wheel.

If I feel tomorrow, like I feel today,
I'll stand right here, look a thousand miles away.

If the blues was whisky, I'd stay drunk all the time,
Stay drunk, baby, just to wear you off my mind.

I got the blues so bad it hurts my feet to walk,
I got the blues so bad, it hurts my tongue to talk.

The blues jumped a rabbit, run him a solid mile,
When the blues overtaken him, he hollered like a newborn
child.

Black American Poets

PHILLIS WHEATLEY (c. 1753–94), born in Senegal, was captured and sold into slavery in early childhood and brought to Boston in 1761. She became the property of John Wheatley whose wife and daughter soon noted her sensitivity and encouraged her to acquire learning. Within a few years she was completely at home in the language and literature of her captors and began writing poetry. She was given her freedom and sent to England when her health began to fail. It was in London where she became a success, and her first poems were published under the title *Poems on Various Subjects, Religious and Moral* (1773).

From TO THE RIGHT HONORABLE WILLIAM, EARL OF DARTMOUTH, HIS MAJESTY'S PRINCIPAL SECRETARY OF STATE FOR NORTH AMERICA, ETC.

. . . .

Should you, my lord, while you pursue my song
Wonder from whence my love of *Freedom* sprung,
Whence flow these wishes for the common good,
By feeling hearts alone best understood,
I, young in life, by seeming cruel fate
Was snatch'd from *Afric's* fancy'd happy seat:
What pangs excruciating must molest,
What sorrows labour in my parent's breast?
Steel'd was the soul and by no misery mov'd
That from a father seiz'd his babe belov'd

Such, such my case. And can I then but pray
Others may never feel tyrannic sway?

. . . .

ON BEING BROUGHT FROM AFRICA
TO AMERICA

'Twas mercy brought me from my *Pagan* land,
Taught my benighted soul to understand
That there's a God, that there's a *Saviour* too;
Once I redemption neither sought nor knew.
Some view our sable race with scornful eye,
"Their color is a diabolic die."
Remember, *Christians, Negroes,* black as *Cain,*
May be refined, and join th' angelic train.

FRANCES E. W. HARPER (1825–1911), born in Baltimore,
Maryland, was both an abolitionist and poet. Her books of poetry
include *Poems on Miscellaneous Subjects* (1854), *Poems* (1871),
and *Sketches of Southern Life* (1872).

THE SLAVE AUCTION

The sale began—young girls were there,
    Defenceless in their wretchedness,
Whose stifled sobs of deep despair
    Revealed their anguish and distress.

And mothers stood with streaming eyes,
    And saw their dearest children sold;
Unheeded rose their bitter cries,
    While tyrants bartered them for gold.

And woman, with her love and truth—
    For these in sable forms may dwell—

Gaz'd on the husband of her youth,
    With anguish none may paint or tell.

And men, whose sole crime was their hue,
    The impress of their Maker's hand,
And frail and shrinking children, too,
    Were gathered in that mournful band.

Ye who have laid your love to rest,
    And wept above their lifeless clay,
Know not the anguish of that breast,
    Whose lov'd are rudely torn away.

Ye may not know how desolate
    Are bosoms rudely forced to part,
And how a dull and heavy weight
    Will press the life-drops from the heart.

JAMES WELDON JOHNSON (1871–1938), born in Jacksonville, Florida, was a leader of the Negro Awakening. He was the first Negro since Reconstruction to be admitted to the bar in Florida. He was a public-school principal, lawyer, diplomat, executive secretary of the National Association for the Advancement of Colored People, and Professor of Creative Literature at Fisk University. His long list of published works includes *Fifty Years and Other Poems* (1917), *God's Trombones* (1927), *St. Peter Relates an Incident of the Resurrection Day* (1930), *The Autobiography of an Ex-Coloured Man* (1912), and an anthology, *Book of American Negro Poetry* (1922). He also collaborated with his brother J. Rosamond Johnson on the classic collection of Negro folk music, *The Book of Negro Spirituals*.

O BLACK AND UNKNOWN BARDS

O black and unknown bards of long ago,
How came your lips to touch the sacred fire?

How, in your darkness, did you come to know
The power and beauty of the minstrel's lyre?
Who first from midst his bonds lifted his eyes?
Who first from out the still watch, lone and long,
Feeling the ancient faith of prophets rise
Within his dark-kept soul, burst into song?

Heart of what slave poured out such melody
As "Steal away to Jesus"? On its strains
His spirit must have nightly floated free,
Though still about his hands he felt his chains.
Who heard great "Jordan roll"? Whose starward eye
Saw chariot "swing low"? And who was he
That breathed that comforting, melodic sigh,
"Nobody know the trouble I see"?

What merely living clod, what captive thing,
Could up toward God through all its darkness grope,
And find within its deadened heart to sing
These songs of sorrow, love and faith, and hope?
How did it catch that subtle undertone,
That note in music heard not with the ears?
How sound the elusive reed so seldom blown,
Which stirs the soul or melts the heart to tears.

Not that great German master in his dream
Of harmonies that thundered amongst the stars
At the creation, ever heard a theme
Nobler than "Go down, Moses." Mark its bars,
How like a mighty trumpet-call they stir
The blood. Such are the notes that men have sung
Going to valorous deeds; such tones there were
That helped make history when Time was young.

There is a wide, wide wonder in it all,
That from degraded rest and servile toil
The fiery spirit of the seer should call

These simple children of the sun and soil.
O black slave singers, gone, forgot, unfamed,
You—you alone, of all the long, long line
Of those who've sung untaught, unknown, unnamed,
Have stretched out upward, seeking the divine.

You sang not deeds of heroes or of kings;
No chant of bloody war, no exulting paean
Of arms-won triumphs; but your humble strings
You touched in chord with music empyrean.
You sang far better than you knew; the songs
That for your listeners' hungry hearts sufficed
Still live—but more than this to you belongs:
You sang a race from wood and stone to Christ.

—1917

PAUL LAURENCE DUNBAR (1872–1906), born in Dayton,
Ohio, was the son of former slaves. He was employed as an eleva-
tor operator when his early books of poetry came out. His third
book, *Lyrics of Lowly Life* (1896), gained for him the national
reputation that enabled him to pursue a literary career. His published books include *Oak and Ivy* (1893), *Majors and Minors*
(1895), *Lyrics of Love and Laughter* (1903), *Lyrics of Sunshine
and Shadow* (1905), and *Complete Poems* (1913).

WE WEAR THE MASK

We wear the mask that grins and lies,
It hides our cheeks and shades our eyes—
This debt we pay to human guile;
With torn and bleeding hearts we smile,
And mouth with myriad subtleties.

Why should the world be otherwise,
In counting all our tears and sighs?

Nay, let them only see us while
    We wear the mask.

We smile, but, O great Christ, our cries
To thee from tortured souls arise.
We sing, but oh the clay is vile
Beneath our feet, and long the mile;
But let the world dream otherwise,
    We wear the mask.

GEORGIA DOUGLAS JOHNSON (1886–1967), born in At-
lanta, Georgia, has several volumes of published verse including
The Heart of a Woman (1918), *Bronze* (1922), and *An Autumn
Love Cycle* (1928).

COMMON DUST

And who shall separate the dust
Which later we shall be:
Whose keen discerning eye will scan
And solve the mystery?

The high, the low, the rich, the poor,
The black, the white, the red,
And all the chromatique between,
Of whom shall it be said:

Here lies the dust of Africa;
Here are the sons of Rome;
Here lies one unlabelled
The world at large his home!

Can one then separate the dust,
Will mankind lie apart,
When life has settled back again
The same as from the start?

INTERRACIAL

Let's build bridges here and there
Or sometimes, just a spiral stair
That we may come somewhat abreast
And sense what cannot be exprest,
And by these measures can be found
A meeting place—a common ground
Nearer the reaches of the heart
Where truth revealed stands clear, apart;
With understanding come to know
What laughing lips will never show:
How tears and torturing distress
May masquerade as happiness.
Then you will know when my heart's aching
And I when yours is slowly breaking.
Commune— The altars will reveal . . .
We then shall be impulsed to kneel
And send a prayer upon its way
For those who wear the thorns today.

Oh, let's build bridges everywhere
And span the gulf of challenge there.

FENTON JOHNSON (1888–1958), born in Chicago, was active
in local literary circles. His published works include *A Little
Dreaming* (1914), *Visions of the Dusk* (1916), *Songs of the Soil*
(1916), and an unpublished collection of his poems in manuscript
is at Fisk University Library.

TIRED

I am tired of work; I am tired of building up somebody else's
civilization.

Let us take a rest, M'Lissy Jane.
I will go down to the Last Chance Saloon, drink a gallon or
    two of gin, shoot a game or two of dice and sleep the rest
        of the night on one of Mike's barrels.
You will let the old shanty go to rot, the white people's
    clothes turn to dust, and the Calvary Baptist Church
        sink to the bottomless pit.

You will spend your days forgetting you married me and your
    nights hunting the warm gin Mike serves the ladies in
        the rear of the Last Chance Saloon.
Throw the children into the river; civilization has given us
    too many. It is better to die than it is to grow up and
        find out that you are colored.
Pluck the stars out of the heavens. The stars mark our destiny.
        The stars marked my destiny.
I am tired of civilization.

JEAN TOOMER (1894–1967), born in Washington, D. C., was
a forerunner of the Negritude movement. His classic *Cane* (1923)
has recently been rediscovered by literary critics. However, of race
Toomer said: "I am of no particular race. I am of the human
race, a man at large in the human world, preparing a new race."

BEEHIVE

Within this black hive to-night
There swarm a million bees;
Bees passing in and out the moon,
Bees escaping out the moon,
Bees returning through the moon,
Silver bees intently buzzing,
Silver honey dripping from the swarm of bees.
Earth is a waxen cell of the world comb,

And I, a drone,
Lying on my back,
Lipping honey,
Getting drunk with silver honey,
Wish that I might fly out past the moon
And curl forever in some far-off farmyard flower.

FRANK HORNE, born in 1899 in New York City, first came to
attention as a poet when his *Letters Found Near a Suicide* won a
Crisis award in 1925. His poems appear in every major anthology, and a small volume of his verse was recently published in
England.

ON SEEING TWO BROWN BOYS
IN A CATHOLIC CHURCH

It is fitting that you be here,
Little brown boys
With Christ-like eyes
And curling hair.

Look you on yonder crucifix
Where He hangs nailed and pierced
With head hung low
And eyes all blind with blood that drips
From a thorny crown . . .
Look you well,
You shall know this thing.

Judas' kiss shall burn your cheek
And you will be denied
By your Peter—

And Gethsemane . . .
You shall know full well . . .
Gethsemane . . .

You, too, will suffer under Pontius Pilate
And feel the rugged cut of rough-hewn cross
Upon your surging shoulder—

They will spit in your face
And laugh . . .
They will nail you up twixt thieves
And gamble for your garments.

And in this you will exceed God
For on this earth
You shall know Hell—

O little brown boys
With Christ-like eyes
And curling hair,
It is fitting that you be here.

MELVIN B. TOLSON (1900–66), born in Moberly, Missouri,
was acclaimed a major poet when his last book, *Harlem Gallery*
(1965), was published. His other books of poetry include *Rendezvous with America* (1944), and *Libretto for Republic of Liberia*
(1953).

from HARLEM GALLERY

*The night John Henry is born an ax
of lightning splits the sky,
and a hammer of thunder pounds the earth,
and the eagles and panthers cry!*

.   .   .

Wafer Waite—
an ex-peon from the Brazos Bottoms,
who was in the M.-K.-T. station
when a dipping funnel

canyoned the Cotton Market Capital—
leaps to his feet and shouts,
"Didn't John Henry's Ma and Pa
get no warning?"

Hideho,
with the tolerance of Diogenes
naked in the market place on a frosty morning,
replies:
"Brother,
the tornado alarm became
tongue-tied."

.   .   .

John Henry—he says to his Ma and Pa:
"Get a gallon of barleycorn.
I want to start right, like a he-man child,
the night that I am born!"

.   .   .

The Zulu Club patrons whoop and stomp,
clap thighs and backs and knees:
the poet and the audience one,
each gears itself to please.

Says: "I want some ham hocks, ribs, and jowls,
a pot of cabbage and greens;
some hoecackes, jam, and buttermilk,
a platter of pork and beans!"

John Henry's Ma—she wrings her hands,
and his Pa—he scratches his head.
John Henry—he curses in giraffe-tall words,
flops over, and kicks down the bed.

He's burning made, like a bear on fire—
so he tears to the riverside.
As he stoops to drink, Old Man River gets scared
and runs upstream to hide!

Some say he was born in Georgia—O Lord!
Some say in Alabam.
But it's writ on the rock at the Big Bend Tunnel:
"Lousyana was my home. So scram!"

. . .

The Zulu Club Wits
(dusky vestiges of the University Wits)
screech like a fanfare of hunting horns
when Hideho flourishes his hip-pocket bottle.

High as the ace of trumps,
an egghead says, " 'The artist is a strange bird,' Lenin says."
Dipping in every direction like a quaquaversal,
the M. C. guffaws: "Hideho, that swig would make
a squirrel spit in the eye of a bulldog!"

Bedlam beggars
at a poet's feast in a people's dusk of dawn counterpoint
protest and pride
in honky-tonk rhythms
hot as an ache in a cold hand warmed.
The creative impulse in the Zulu Club
leaps from Hideho's lips to Frog Legs' fingers,
like the electric fire from the clouds
that blued the gap between
Franklin's key and his Leyden jar.
A Creole co-ed from Basin Street by way of
Morningside Heights
—circumspect as a lady in waiting—
brushes my shattered cocktail glass into a tray.
Am I a Basilidian anchoret rapt in secret studies?
O spiritual, work-song, ragtime, blues, jazz—
consorts of
the march, quadrille, polka, and waltz!

Witness to a miracle
—I muse—
the birth of a blues,
the flesh
made André Gide's
musique nègre!

. . .

I was born in Bitchville, Lousyana.
A son of Ham, I had to scram!
I was born in Bitchville, Lousyana;
so I ain't worth a T.B. damn!

. . .

My boon crony,
Vincent Aveline, sports editor
of the *Harlem Gazette,*
anchors himself at my table.
"What a night!" he groans. "*What* a night!"
. . . I wonder . . .
Was he stewed or not
when he sneaked Hideho's
Skid Row Ballads
from my walk-up apartment?
Then the You advises the I,
Every bookworm is a potential thief.

. . .

Ma taught me to pray. Pa taught me to grin.
It pays, Black Boy; oh, it pays!
So I pray to God and grin at the Whites
in seventy-seven different ways!

I came to Lenox Avenue.
Poor Boy Blue! Poor Boy Blue!
I came to Lenox Avenue,
but I find up here a Bitchville, too!

. . .

Like an explorer
on the deck of the *Albatross,*
ex-professor of philosophy, Joshua Nitze,
sounds the wet unknown;
then, in humor, he refreshes the Zulu Club Wits
with an anecdote on integration,
from the Athens of the Cumberland:
"A black stevedore bulked his butt
in a high-hat restaurant
not far from the bronze equestrian statue
of Andrew Jackson.
The ofay waitress hi-fied,
'What can I do for you, Mister?'
Imagine, if you can, Harlem nitwits,
a black man mistered by a white dame
in the Bible Belt of the pale phallus and the chalk clitoris!
The South quaked.
Gabriel hadn't high-Ced his horn,
nor the Africans invaded from Mars.
It was only the end-man's bones of Jeff Davis
rattling the *Dies Irae*
in the Hollywood Cemetery!
The Negro dock hand said,
'Ma'am, a platter of chitterlings.'
The ofay waitress smiled a blond dolichocephalic smile,
'That's not on the menu, Mister.'
Then the stevedore sneered:
'Night and day, Ma'am,
I've been telling Black Folks
you White Folks ain't ready for integration!' "

STERLING A. BROWN, born in 1901 in Washington, D. C., is a leading authority on Negro folklore. His anthology *The Negro Caravan* (1941) remains one of the best of its kind, and he has also published *Southern Road* (1932), *The Negro in American Fiction,* and *Negro Poetry and Drama*. His poetry appears in numerous anthologies.

STRANGE LEGACIES

One thing you left with us, Jack Johnson.
One thing before they got you.

You used to stand there like a man,
Taking punishment
With a golden, spacious grin;
Confident.
Inviting big Jim Jeffries, who was boring in:
"Heah ah is, big boy; yuh sees whah Ise at.
Come on in. . . ."

Thanks, Jack, for that.

John Henry, with your hammer;
John Henry, with your steel driver's pride,
You taught us that a man could go down like a man,
Sticking to your hammer till you died.
Sticking to your hammer till you died.

Brother,
When, beneath the burning sun
The sweat poured down and the breath came thick,
And the loaded hammer swung like a ton
And the heart grew sick;
You had what we need now, John Henry.
Help us get it.

So if we go down
Have to go down

We go like you, brother,
'Nachal' men. . . .

Old nameless couple in Red River Bottom,
Who have seen floods gutting out your best loam,
And the boll weevil chase you
Out of your hard-earned home,
Have seen the drought parch your green fields,
And the cholera stretch your porkers out dead;
Have seen year after year
The commissary always a little in the lead;
Even you said
That which we need
Now in our time of fear,—
Routed your own deep misery and dread,
Muttering, beneath an unfriendly sky,
"Guess we'll give it one mo' try.
Guess we'll give it one mo' try."

STRONG MEN

> *The strong men keep coming on.*
> —Sandburg

They dragged you from the homeland,
They chained you in coffles,
They huddled you spoon-fashion in filthy hatches,
They sold you to give a few gentlemen ease.

They broke you in like oxen,
They scourged you,
They branded you,
They made your women breeders,
They swelled your numbers with bastards . . . . .
They taught you the religion they disgraced.
You sang:

> Keep a-inchin' along
> Lak a po' inch worm . . .

You sang:
> By and bye
> I'm gonna lay down this heaby load . . .

You sang:
> Walk togedder, chillen,
> Dontcha git weary . . .
>> The strong men keep a-comin' on
>> The strong men get stronger.

They point with pride to the roads you built for them,
They ride in comfort over the rails you laid for them.
They put hammers in your hands
And said—Drive so much before sundown.
You sang:
> Ain't no hammah
> In dis lan'
> Strikes lak mine, bebby,
> Strikes lak mine.

They cooped you in their kitchens,
They penned you in their factories,
They gave you the jobs that they were too good for,
They tried to guarantee happiness to themselves
By shunting dirt and misery to you.
You sang:
> Me an' muh baby gonna shine, shine
> Me an' muh baby gonna shine.
>> The strong men keep a-comin' on
>> The strong men git stronger . . .

They bought off some of your leaders
You stumbled, as blind men will . . .
They coaxed you, unwontedly soft-voiced . . .
You followed a way.
Then laughed as usual.
They heard the laugh and wondered;
Uncomfortable;

Unadmitting a deeper terror . . .
　　　　　The strong men keep a-comin' on
　　　　　Gittin' stronger . . .

What, from the slums
Where they have hemmed you,
What, from the tiny huts
They could not keep from you—
What reaches them
Making them ill at ease, fearful?
Today they shout prohibition at you
"Thou shalt not this"
"Thou shalt not that"
"Reserved for whites only"
You laugh.

One thing they cannot prohibit—

　　　　　The strong men . . . coming on
　　　　　The strong men gittin' stronger.
　　　　　Strong men . . .
　　　　　Stronger . . .

OLD LEM

I talked to old Lem
and old Lem said:
　　　　"They weigh the cotton
　　　　They store the corn
　　　　　　We only good enough
　　　　　　To work the rows;
　　　　They run the commissary
　　　　They keep the books
　　　　　　We gotta be grateful
　　　　　　For being cheated;
　　　　Whippersnapper clerks

Call us out of our name
    We got to say mister
    To spindling boys
They make our figgers
Turn somersets
We buck in the middle
    Say, "Thankyuh, sah."
        They don't come by ones
        They don't come by twos
        But they come by tens.

"They got the judges
They got the lawyers
They got the jury-rolls
They got the law
        They don't come by ones
They got the sheriffs
They got the deputies
        They don't come by twos
They got the shotguns
They got the rope
    We git the justice
    In the end
        And they come by tens.

"Their fists stay closed
Their eyes look straight
    Our hands stay open
    Our eyes must fall
        They don't come by ones
They got the manhood
They got the courage
        They don't come by twos
    We got to slink around
    Hangtailed hounds.
They burn us when we dogs

They burn us when we men
　　　　They come by tens . . .

"I had a buddy
Six foot of man
Muscled up perfect
Game to the heart
　　　　They don't come by ones
Outworked and outfought
Any man or two men
　　　　They don't come by twos
He spoke out of turn
At the commissary
They gave him a day
To git out the county.
He didn't take it.
He said 'Come and get me.'
They came and got him
　　　　And they came by tens.
He stayed in the county—
He lays there dead.

　　　　　They don't come by ones
　　　　　They don't come by twos
　　　　　But they come by tens."

ARNA BONTEMPS, born in 1902 in Alexandria, Louisiana, is one of the most distinguished Negro literary figures. He was for many years Head Librarian at Fisk University, has taught at the Chicago Circle campus of the University of Illinois, and is now Curator of the James Weldon Johnson Collection at Yale University Library. He has written many different types of books, poetry, history, novels, and compiled various anthologies. Among his books are *Black Thunder* (1936), *Story of the Negro* (1958), *One Hundred Years of Negro Freedom* (1961), and a volume of poetry entitled *Personals* (1963). His anthologies of poetry are *Golden Slippers* (1941), *American Negro Poetry* (1963), and he collaborated with the late Langston Hughes on the important *The Poetry of the Negro* (1949 and revised 1969).

SOUTHERN MANSION

Poplars are standing there still as death
And ghosts of dead men
Meet their ladies walking
Two by two beneath the shade
And standing on the marble steps.

There is a sound of music echoing
Through the open door
And in the field there is
Another sound tinkling in the cotton:
Chains of bondmen dragging on the ground.

The years go back with an iron clank,
A hand is on the gate,
A dry leaf trembles on the wall.
Ghosts are walking.
They have broken roses down
And poplars stand there still as death.

LANGSTON HUGHES (1902–67), born in Joplin, Missouri, is the world's most famous black writer. His poetry has been translated into every major language. *The Weary Blues* (1926) was the first and *The Panther and the Lash* (1967) was the last of his ten volumes of published poetry.

THE NEGRO SPEAKS OF RIVERS

I've known rivers:
I've known rivers ancient as the world and older than the
                          flow of human blood in human veins.
My soul has grown deep like the rivers.
I bathed in the Euphrates when dawns were young.
I built my hut near the Congo and it lulled me to sleep.
I looked upon the Nile and raised the pyramids above it.
I heard the singing of the Mississippi when Abe Lincoln went
     down to New Orleans, and I've seen its muddy bosom
                          turn all golden in the sunset.
I've known rivers:
Ancient, dusky rivers.
My soul has grown deep like the rivers.

MOTHER TO SON

Well, son, I'll tell you:
Life for me ain't been no crystal stair.
It's had tacks in it,
And splinters,
And boards torn up,
And places with no carpet on the floor—
Bare.
But all the time
I'se been a-climbin' on,
And reachin' landin's,
And turnin' corners,

And sometimes goin' in the dark
Where there ain't been no light.
So boy, don't you turn back.
Don't you set down on the steps
'Cause you finds it's kinder hard.
Don't you fall now—
For I'se still goin', honey,
I'se still climbin',
And life for me ain't been no crystal stair.

TRUMPET PLAYER

The Negro
With the trumpet at his lips
Has dark moons of weariness
Beneath his eyes
Where the smouldering memory
Of slave ships
Blazed to the crack of whips
About his thighs.

The Negro
With the trumpet at his lips
Has a head of vibrant hair
Tamed down,
Patent-leathered now
Until it gleams
Like jet—
Were jet a crown.

The music
From the trumpet at his lips
Is honey
Mixed with liquid fire.

The rhythm
From the trumpet at his lips
Is ecstasy
Distilled from old desire—

Desire
That is longing for the moon
Where the moonlight's but a spotlight
In his eyes,
Desire
That is longing for the sea
Where sea's a bar-glass
Sucker size.

The Negro
With the trumpet at his lips
Whose jacket
Has a *fine* one-button roll,
Does not know
Upon what riff the music slips
Its hypodermic needle
To his soul—

But softly
As the tune comes from his throat
Trouble
Mellows to a golden note.

HARLEM SWEETIES

Have you dug the spill
Of Sugar Hill?
Cast your gims
On this sepia thrill:
Brown sugar lassie,

Caramel treat,
Honey-gold baby
Sweet enough to eat.
Peach-skinned girlie,
Coffee and cream,
Chocolate darling
Out of a dream.
Walnut tinted
Or cocoa brown,
Pomegranate-lipped
Pride of the town.
Rich cream-colored
To plum-tinted black,
Feminine sweetness
In Harlem's no lack.
Glow of the quince
To blush of the rose.
Persimmon bronze
To cinnamon toes.
Blackberry cordial,
Virginia Dare wine—
All those sweet colors
Flavor Harlem of mine!
Walnut or cocoa,
Let me repeat:
Caramel, brown sugar,
A chocolate treat.

WHEN SUE WEARS RED

When Susanna Jones wears red
Her face is like an ancient cameo
Turned down by the ages.

Come with a blast of trumpets,
        Jesus!

When Susanna Jones wears red
A queen from some time-dead Egyptian night
Walks once again.

Blow trumpets, Jesus!

And the beauty of Susanna Jones in red
Burns in my heart a love-fire sharp like pain.

Sweet silver trumpets,
        Jesus!

WITHOUT BENEFIT OF
DECLARATION

Listen here, Joe
Don't you know
That tomorrow
You got to go
Out yonder where
The steel winds blow?

Listen here, kid,
It's been said
Tomorrow you'll be dead
Out there where
The snow is lead.

Don't ask me why.
Just go ahead and die.
Hidden from the sky
Out yonder you'll lie:
A medal to your family—
In exchange for
A guy.

Mama, don't cry.

ANGOLA QUESTION MARK

Don't know why I,
Black,
Must still stand
With my back
To the last frontier
Of fear
In my own land.

Don't know why I
Now must turn
Into a Mau Mau
And lift my hand
Against my fellow man
To live on my own land.

But it is so—
And being so
I know
For you and me
There's woe.

COUNTEE CULLEN (1903–46), born in New York City, was
one of the most famous writers of the Harlem Renaissance. His
volumes of poetry include *Color* (1925), *The Ballad of the Brown
Girl* and *Copper Sun* (1927), *The Black Christ* (1929), *The Medea
and Other Poems* (1935), and *On These I Stand* (1947).

HERITAGE

for Harold Jackman

What is Africa to me:
Copper sun or scarlet sea,
Jungle star or jungle track,

Strong bronzed men, or regal black
Women from whose loins I sprang
When the birds of Eden sang?
One three centuries removed
From the scenes his fathers loved,
Spicy grove, cinnamon tree,
What is Africa to me?

So I lie, who all day long
Want no sound except the song
Sung by wild barbaric birds
Goading massive jungle herds,
Juggernauts of flesh that pass
Trampling tall defiant grass
Where young forest lovers lie,
Plighting troth beneath the sky.
So I lie, who always hear,
Though I cram against my ear
Both my thumbs, and keep them there,
Great drums throbbing through the air.
So I lie, whose fount of pride,
Dear distress, and joy allied,
Is my somber flesh and skin,
With the dark blood dammed within
Like great pulsing tides of wine
That, I fear, must burst the fine
Channels of the chafing net
Where they surge and foam and fret.

Africa? A book one thumbs
Listlessly, till slumber comes.
Unremembered are her bats
Circling through the night, her cats
Crouching in the river reeds,
Stalking gentle flesh that feeds
By the river brink; no more

Does the bugle-throated roar
Cry that monarch claws have leapt
From the scabbards where they slept.
Silver snakes that once a year
Doff the lovely coats you wear,
See no covert in your fear
Lest a mortal eye should see;
What's your nakedness to me?
Here no leprous flowers rear
Fierce corollas in the air;
Here no bodies sleek and wet,
Dripping mingled rain and sweat,
Tread the savage measures of
Jungle boys and girls in love.
What is last year's snow to me,
Last year's anything? The tree
Budding yearly must forget
How its past arose or set—
Bough and blossom, flower, fruit,
Even what shy bird with mute
Wonder at her travail there,
Meekly labored in its hair.
One three centuries removed,
From the scenes his fathers loved,
Spicy grove, cinnamon tree,
What is Africa to me?

So I lie, who find no peace
Night or day, no slight release
From the unremittent beat
Made by cruel padded feet
Walking through my body's street.
Up and down they go, and back,
Treading out a jungle track.
So I lie, who never quite

Safely sleep from rain at night—
I can never rest at all
When the rain begins to fall;
Like a soul gone bad with pain
I must match its weird refrain;
Ever must I twist and squirm,
Writhing like a baited worm,
While its primal measures drip
Through my body, crying, "Strip!
Doff this new exuberance.
Come and dance the Lover's Dance!"
In an old remembered way
Rain works on me night and day.

Quaint, outlandish heathen gods
Black men fashion out of rods,
Clay, and brittle bits of stone,
In a likeness like their own,
My conversion came high-priced;
I belong to Jesus Christ,
Preacher of humility;
Heathen gods are naught to me.
Father, Son, and Holy Ghost,
So I make an idle boast;
Jesus of the twice-turned cheek,
Lamb of God, although I speak
With my mouth thus, in my heart
Do I play a double part.

Ever at Thy glowing altar
Must my heart grow sick and falter,
Wishing He I served were black,
Thinking then it would not lack
Precedent of pain to guide it,
Let who would or might deride it;
Surely then this flesh would know

Yours had borne a kindred woe.
Lord, I fashion dark gods, too,
Daring even to give You
Dark despairing features where,
Crowned with dark rebellious hair,
Patience wavers just so much as
Mortal grief compels, while touches
Quick and hot, of anger, rise
To smitten cheek and weary eyes.
Lord, forgive me if my need
Sometimes shapes a human creed.
All day long and all night through,
One thing only must I do:
Quench my pride and cool my blood,
Lest I perish in the flood.
Lest a hidden ember set
Timber that I thought was wet
Burning like the dryest flax,
Melting like the merest wax,
Lest the grave restore its dead.
Not yet has my heart or head
In the least way realized
They and I are civilized.

FOR A POET

I have wrapped my dreams in a silken cloth,
And laid them away in a box of gold;
Where long will cling the lips of the moth,
I have wrapped my dreams in a silken cloth;
I hide no hate; I am not even wroth
Who found earth's breath so keen and cold;
I have wrapped my dreams in a silken cloth,
And laid them away in a box of gold.

YET DO I MARVEL

I doubt not God is good, well-meaning, kind,
And did He stoop to quibble could tell why

The little buried mole continues blind,
Why flesh that mirrors Him must someday die,
Make plain the reason tortured Tantalus
Is baited by the fickle fruit, declare
If merely brute caprice dooms Sisyphus
To struggle up a never-ending stair.

Inscrutable His ways are, and immune
To catchesim by a mind too strewn
With petty cares to slightly understand
What awful brain compels His awful hand;
Yet do I marvel at this curious thing:
To make a poet black, and bid him sing!

SIMON THE CYRENIAN SPEAKS

He never spoke a word to me,
And yet He called my name;
He never gave a sign to me,
And yet I knew and came.

At first I said, "I will not bear
His cross upon my back;
He only seeks to place it there
Because my skin is black."

But He was dying for a dream,
And He was very meek,
And in His eyes there shone a gleam
Men journey far to seek.

It was Himself my pity bought;
I did for Christ alone
When all of Rome could not have wrought
With bruise of lash or stone.

WARING CUNEY, born in Washington, D. C. in 1906, is a
musician as well as poet. His poem *No Images* is one of the most
widely anthologized by a black poet.

MY LORD, WHAT A MORNING

Oh, my Lord
What a morning,
Oh, my Lord,
What a feeling,
When Jack Johnson
Turned Jim Jeffries'
Snow-white face
Up to the ceiling.
Yes, my Lord,
Fighting is wrong,
But what an uppercut.
Oh, my Lord,
What a morning.
Oh, my Lord
What a feeling,
When Jack Johnson
Turned Jim Jeffries'
Lily-white face
Up to the ceiling.
Oh, my Lord
What a morning,
Oh, my Lord
Take care of Jack.
Keep him, Lord
As you made him,
Big, and strong, and black.

NO IMAGES

She does not know
Her beauty,
She thinks her brown body
Has no glory.

If she could dance
Naked,
Under palm trees
And see her image in the river
She would know.

But there are no palm trees
On the street,
And dish water gives back no images.

ROBERT HAYDEN, born in 1913 in Detroit, Michigan, is winner of many awards and grants including The Hopwood Award
(1938), Rosenwald Fellowship (1947), Ford Foundation grant
(1954), and Grand Prize for Poetry at First World Festival of Negro Arts at Dakar, Senegal (1965). His published books of poetry
include *Heart-Shape in the Dust* (1940), *A Ballad of Remem-
brance* (1962), and *Selected Poems* (1966).

FREDERICK DOUGLASS

When it is finally ours, this freedom, this liberty, this
                                          beautiful
and terrible thing, needful to man as air,
usable as earth; when it belongs at last to all,
when it is truly instinct, brain matter, diastole, systole,
reflex action; when it is finally won; when it is more
than the gaudy mumbo jumbo of politicians:
this man, this Douglass, this former slave, this Negro

beaten to his knees, exiled, visioning a world
where none is lonely, none hunted, alien,
this man, superb in love and logic, this man
shall be remembered. Oh, not with statues' rhetoric,
not with legends and poems and wreaths of bronze alone,
but with the lives grown out of his life, the lives
fleshing his dream of the beautiful, needful thing.

OWEN DODSON, born in 1914 in Brooklyn, New York, long
time chairman of the Drama Department of Howard University,
has distinguished himself both as poet and playwright. He has
published a book of poems, *Powerful Long Ladder* (1946), and
two novels.

THE CONFESSION STONE
A Song Cycle
Sung by Mary about Jesus

I.
Oh my boy: Jesus,
My first and only son,
Rock on my breast
My first and only one.
My first and only son.
Oh my Jesus:
My first and only one:
Born of God and born
near His sun
Bright boy: My only one:
Oh my Jesus
Rest on my breast
My first and only son:
Oh my boy Jesus: rest.
Shushhh, you need the rest.

II.
Don't pay attention
To the old men in the Temple:
They have given up.
Tell them what you told me:
Cast the sinners out,
Clean the house of God,
Load the rich with grief,
Prepare the poor with hope . . .
. . . and Jesus
Don't stop to play
With Judas and his friends
Along the way.

III.
Jesus, did you know
That Lazarus is back?
Jesus, are you listening:
Lazarus has come back.
His grave is still open
And Martha tells she heard
Three angels singing
With three birds:
Their feathers brushed together.
Jesus, are you hearing:
Lazarus has returned
To Bethany.
Jesus, won't you answer:
Lazarus has come back
And he's calling for you
He says that death was gentle
And woke him up early.
Jesus, are you praying:
Lazarus has returned.

IV.
There's a supper in Jerusalem tonight
And I wish that I was there
I'd journey anywhere
To be with Jesus:
To stroke His hair,
Remind Him, oh my baby dear,
I'd journey anywhere
To be with Jesus tonight.
There's that supper in Jerusalem tonight
And I could be right there.
But I don't dare
To venture to Jerusalem tonight.
Oh my Jesus you're eating in Jerusalem tonight
And I wish that I was there.
Oh my boy take care
At that supper in Jerusalem tonight.

V.
Cold and icy in my bed:
Layed on the ground of Jerusalem:
Every flower is withered,
The birds have left their song,
The sun wears a twisted eye.
I'm alone with Your dream of redemption
My Lord . . . save Him, save our son.

I'm His mother: save Him:
Let me rock Him again in my trembling arms.
Save Him. I'll receive the silver from Judas.
Help Him. Your word is all my world.
I'll receive the silver from Judas' hand
And spend it on . . . nothing . . .
Save Him . . . Jehovah,
Help Him . . . my God,
Bless Him . . . my Lord,

Redeem Him, my Husband.
Oh save Him, save Him, save Him,
Save Him, save our boy!

VI.
Bring me those needles, Martha,
I believe I'll knot Jesus a scarf.
Go on snapping those butterbeans . . .
What time is it?
Let me see now: knit one . . .
You say it's twelve o'clock?
Snap enough for Joseph and Lazarus:
They'll be home before you're through.
Martha, what time is it? Purl two . . .
Purl one,
Knit one,
Purl two . . .
If I had the star of Bethlehem . . .
I'd knit three . . .
. . . and light His sky . . .
Where was I, Martha?
Oh yes, knit one,
Purl seven . . .
What time is it, Martha?
Knit three . . . purl ten . . .
It can't be near three o'clock.
Where was I? Knit . . . purl twelve . . .
Purl nothing . . .
Martha, don't leave me alone.
Where are you, Martha?
Martha, where are you, Martha?
Martha!

VII.
Everything is black:
Air, water, sun, moon,

All light . . . dirt is black.
Heaven is in mourning for our Son.
The earth is dead:
It will light again
Almighty God.
Now I understand
What light is:
It is our Son.
It is Jesus, no longer trembling
In my arms: it is THE CHRIST.
Oh my boy Jesus
My first and only one.
Now on my knees, with Joseph at my side,
I ask Thee: send the resurrection now.
Give the air and water and the sun
And the moon and the dirt: Thy light again.
Send the presence, Almighty God,
Send it even to evil men.
I see Jesus in the clouds
OH OH OH OH OH oh oh oh ohooooo
Free Him from death for life:
We must be free to sing:
Loose the birds for their song,
Bloom the flowers for their songs,
Light Martha, whose brother came back
From death, light Mary Magdalen,
Light Gethsemane's gardens:
Light those walkways with lilies,
And heal the wounds of Christ.
Let me rise up
Into your starry sky
And love our Son,
And PRAISE THEE.
And PRAISE THEE
—Ah comfort me in Paradise.

VIII.
Oh my boy: Jesus,
My first and only Son,
Rock on my breast
My first and only one.
My first and only Son.
Oh my Jesus:
My first and only one:
Born of God and born
        near His sun
Bright boy: My only one:
Oh my Jesus
Rest on my breast
My first and only Son:
Oh my boy Jesus: rest.
Shushhh, you need the rest.

RAY DUREM (1915–63), born in Seattle, Washington, was a member of the International Brigades during the Spanish Civil War. His poems appear in *New Negro Poets: USA* and other anthologies.

AWARD

> *A Gold Watch to the FBI*
> *Man who has followed*
> *me for 25 years.*

Well, old spy
looks like I
led you down some pretty blind alleys,
took you on several trips to Mexico,
fishing in the high Sierras,
jazz at the Philharmonic.

You've watched me all your life,
I've clothed your wife,
put your two sons through college.
what good has it done?
the sun keeps rising every morning.
ever see me buy an Assistant President?
or close a school?
or lend money to Trujillo?
ever catch me rigging airplane prices?
I bought some after-hours whiskey in L.A.
but the Chief got his pay.
I ain't killed no Koreans
or fourteen-year-old boys in Mississippi.
neither did I bomb Guatemala,
or lend guns to shoot Algerians.
I admit I took a Negro child
to a white rest room in Texas,
but she was my daughter, only three,
who had to pee.

SAMUEL ALLEN, born in 1917 in Columbus, Ohio, first came
to prominence when Richard Wright had his poetry published in
Présence Africaine. His collection of poems *Elfenbein Zaehne*
("Ivory Tusks") (1956) was published in Heidelberg, Germany.

TO SATCH*

Sometimes I feel like I will *never* stop
Just go on forever
Till one fine mornin'
I'm gonna reach up and grab me a handfulla stars
Swing out my long lean leg

* The legendary Satchell Paige, one of the star pitchers in Negro baseball

And whip three hot strikes burnin' down the heavens
And look over at God and say,
How about that!

GWENDOLYN BROOKS, born in 1917 in Topeka, Kansas, won the 1950 Pultizer Prize for poetry and is now official Poet Laureate of the state of Illinois where she has spent most of her life. Her collections of published poetry include *A Street in Bronzeville* (1945), *Annie Allen* (1949), *The Bean Eaters* (1960), *Selected Poems* (1963), and *In The Mecca* (1968).

THE BEAN EATERS

They eat beans mostly, this old yellow pair.
Dinner is a casual affair.
Plain chipware on a plain and creaking wood,
Tin flatware.

Two who are Mostly Good.
Two who have lived their day,
But keep on putting on their clothes
And putting things away.

And remembering . . .
Remembering, with twinklings and twinges,
As they lean over the beans in their rented back room
　　　　that is full of beads and receipts and dolls and clothes,
　　　　　　　　tobacco crumbs, vases and fringes.

WE REAL COOL

　　The Pool Players.
　　Seven at the Golden Shovel.

We real cool. We
Left school. We

Lurk late. We
Strike straight. We

Sing sin. We
Thin gin. We

Jazz June. We
Die soon.

MALCOLM X

for Dudley Randall

Original.
Ragged-round.
Rich-robust.

He had the hawk-man's eyes.
We gasped. We saw the maleness.
The maleness raking out and making guttural the air
and pushing us to the walls.

And in a soft and fundamental hour
a sorcery devout and vertical
beguiled the world.

He opened us—
who was a key,

who was a man.

OLIVER PITCHER, born in 1923 in Massachusetts, has a volume of poetry entitled *Dust of Silence* and appears in anthologies in the United States, England, and Germany.

THE PALE BLUE CASKET

Why don't we rock the casket here in the moonlight?

A man begins in the cradle and ends in the casket.
That's if he's a two time winner. In between? The
echo of a long lament. A mosaic of sleep. A marble
laugh. A few grapes. A short wail from the other
shore. The scattered moldly crumbs of best intentions
and the insecure peace of distance. The moon and
the sun go on playing an eternal game Show-me-yours
and I'll-show-you-mine but words fail us. We say,
here lies a man in a telephone booth, already cold
and without direct communication to the moon to
warm himself. And rock so soon!

Rock, rock, rock the casket here in the moonlight.

TED JOANS, born in 1928 on a riverboat in Cairo, Illinois, is a poet, painter, jazz musician. He satirized the "Beat Generation" in a book of cartoons with commentary *The Hipsters* and his poems appear in many anthologies here and abroad.

THE TRUTH

IF YOU SHOULD SEE A MAN
walking down a crowded
street
      talking
         ALOUD

TO HIMSELF
                    DON'T RUN
                              IN THE
OPPOSITE DIRECTION
                         BUT RUN
TOWARD HIM
              for he is a
                         POET
You have NOTHING to
                    FEAR
FROM THE
          POET
                    BUT THE
     TRUTH

     ITS CURTAINS

All god's SPADES wear dark shades
     and some of god's SPADES
(you'll never be able to figger what nigger)
     carry   l   o   n   g   sharp
              protective blades
                         so I repeat, though
he may be raggedy or neat
     All god's SPADES got SHADES

MARTIN LUTHER KING, JR. (1929–68), born in Atlanta, Georgia, more than any other person in recent times, captured the imagination of the black masses as a leader. Although it is not poetry in the formal sense, his famous speech "I Have a Dream," delivered at the 1963 March on Washington, belongs in this collection.

excerpt from I HAVE A DREAM

I have a dream that one day on the red hills of Georgia the sons of slaves and the sons of former slaveowners will be able to sit down together at the table of brotherhood. I have a dream that one day even the state of Mississippi, sweltering with the heat of injustice, sweltering with the heat of oppression, will be transformed into an oasis of freedom and justice.

I have a dream that my four little children will one day live in a Nation where they will not be judged by the color of their skins, but by the conduct and their character.

I have a dream that one day in Alabama, with this vicious racist, its Governor, having his lips dripping the words of interposition and nullification—one day right there in Alabama, little black boys and little black girls will be able to join hands with little white boys and little white girls as brothers and sisters.

I have a dream that one day every valley shall be exalted, every hill and mountain shall be made low, the rough places will be made plane, the crooked places will be made straight and the glory of the Lord shall be revealed and all flesh shall see it together.

This is our hope. This is the faith that I go back to the South with. With this faith, we will be able to hew out of the mountains of despair a stone of hope. With this faith, we will be able to transform the jangling discord of our Nation into a beautiful symphony of brotherhood. With this faith, we will be able to work together; to go to jail together; to stand up for freedom together knowing that we will be free one day . . .

CALVIN HERNTON, born in 1932 in Chattanooga, Tennessee, is one of the most controversial young writers. His books include *Sex and Racism in America* (1964) and *White Papers for White Americans* (1965) and his poetry appears in various anthologies.

THE DISTANT DRUM

I am not a metaphor or symbol.
This you hear is not the wind in the trees,
Nor a cat being maimed in the street.
I am being maimed in the street.
It is I who weep, laugh, feel pain or joy,
Speak this because I exist.
This is my voice.
These words are my words,
My mouth speaks them,
My hand writes—
I am a poet.
It is my fist you hear
Beating against your ear.

LeROI JONES, born in 1934 in Newark, New Jersey, is the leader of a new wave of black writers. His plays *Dutchman, The Slave,* and *The Toilet* have won enthusiastic praise from critics. His published poetry includes *Preface to a Twenty Volume Suicide Note* (1961), *The Dead Lecturer* (1964), and an anthology entitled *Black Fire* (1968).

AUDUBON, DRAFTED
(For Linda)

It does not happen. That love, removes
itself. (I am leaving, Goodbye!)
                    Removes

itself, as rain, hard iron rain
comes down, then stops. All those
eyes opened for morning, close with
what few hours given them. With tears,
or at a stone wall, shadows drag down.

I am what I think I am. You are what
I think you are. The world is the
one thing, that will not move. It is
made of stone, round, and very ugly.

PREFACE TO A TWENTY
VOLUME SUICIDE NOTE

Lately, I've become accustomed to the way
The ground opens up and envelops me
Each time I go out to walk the dog.
Or the broad edged silly music the wind
Makes when I run for a bus—

Things have come to that.

And now, each night I count the stars,
And each night I get the same number.
And when they will not come to be counted
I count the holes they leave.

Nobody sings anymore.

And then, last night, I tiptoed up
To my daughter's room and heard her
Talking to someone, and when I opened
The door, there was no one there . . .
Only she on her knees,
Peeking into her own clasped hands.

BOB KAUFMAN, who was born around 1935 in San Francisco, California, played an important part in the so-called Beat Generation renaissance of the 1950's with Allen Ginsberg, Gregory Corso, and Lawrence Ferlinghetti. He has published a volume of poems entitled *Solitudes Crowded With Loneliness* (1965).

BATTLE REPORT

One thousand saxophones infiltrate the city,
Each with a man inside,
Hidden in ordinary cases,
Labeled FRAGILE.

A fleet of trumpets drop their hooks,
Inside at the outside.

Ten waves of trombones approach the city
Under blue cover
Of late autumn's neo-classical clouds.

Five hundred bassmen, all string feet tall,
Beating it back to the bass.

One hundred drummers, each a stick in each hand,
The delicate rumble of pianos, moving in.

The secret agent, an innocent bystander,
Drops a note in the wail box.

Five generals, gathered in the gallery,
Blowing plans.
At last, the secret code is flashed:
Now is the time, now is the time.

Attack: The sound of jazz.

The city falls.

UNHOLY MISSIONS

I want to be buried in an anonymous crater inside the moon.

I want to build miniature golf courses on all the stars.

I want to prove that Atlantis was a summer resort for cave
                                                        men.

I want to prove that Los Angeles is a practical joked played
            on us by superior beings on a humorous planet.

I want to expose Heaven as an exclusive sanitarium filled
                with rich psychopaths who think they can fly.

I want to show that the Bible was serialized in a Roman
                                        children's magazine.

I want to prove that the sun was born when God fell asleep
        with a lit cigarette, tired after a hard night of judging.

I want to prove once and for all that I am not crazy.

JULIAN BOND, born in 1940 in Nashville, Tennessee, is a
member of the House of Representatives (Georgia) and a poet.
His poems appear in various anthologies including *New Negro
Poets: U.S.A.* and *American Negro Poetry*.

LOOK AT THAT GAL . . .

Look at that gal
    Shake that thing.
We cannot all be
    Martin Luther King . . .

MARI EVANS, born in Toledo, Ohio, is Writer-in-Residence at
Indiana University-Purdue University, Indianapolis, and pro-
ducer/director of a weekly TV show. Her poetry appears in a
number of textbooks and anthologies, including *New Negro
Poets: USA.*

WHERE HAVE YOU GONE ... ?

where have you gone

with your confident
walk   with
your crooked smile

why did you leave
me
when you took your
laughter
and departed

are you aware that
with you
went the sun
all light
and what few stars
there were?

where have you gone
with your confident
walk your
crooked smile the
rent money
in one pocket and
my heart
in
another ...

CAROL FREEMAN, born in 1941 in Rayville, Louisiana, attended Oakland City College and the University of California. Her poetry appears in *Black Fire,* and other anthologies.

CHRISTMAS MORNING I
(For my daughters, Koina and Messiri)

Christmas morning i
got up before the others and
ran
naked across the plank
floor into the front
room to see grandmama
sewing a new
button on my last year
ragdoll.

BOBB HAMILTON is a young sculptor and poet who has been active on the New York scene. He is one of the editors of *Soulbook,* a journal of revolutionary Afro-America.

POEM TO A NIGGER COP

Hey there poleece
Black skin in blue mask
You really gonna uphold the law?
What you gonna do when you see
Your Mama
    Running down 125th street with
A t.v. set tied up in a bandana trying to catch the train to
    Springfield Gardens?
    You mean to tell me you gonna
Bang your own mother?
    Bang! Bang!

I can see you now grinning
    A big black no nuts nigger
On channel number 5
Your teeth rolling across the screen
Like undotted dice
    Talking about how you "uphelt
    De Law."
While Mr. Charlie sticks his white
    Finger up your ass
And pins a little gold medal on your
    Chest!
And then you'll bust out into soft shoe shuffle
    While a background chorus sings
"God Bless America,"
With an Irish accent.

NIKKI GIOVANNI, born in 1943 in Knoxville, Tennessee, attended Fisk University and the University of Pennsylvania. Her published works include *Black Feeling Black Talk* (1968) and *Black Judgement* (1968).

FOR SAUNDRA

i wanted to write
a poem
that rhymes
but revolution doesn't lend
itself to be-bopping

then my neighbor
who thinks i hate
asked—do you ever write
tree poems—i like trees
so i thought

i'll write a beautiful green tree poem
peeked from my window
to check the image
noticed the school yard was covered
with asphalt
no green—no trees grow
in manhattan

then, well, i thought the sky
i'll do a big blue sky poem
but all the clouds have winged
low since no-Dick was elected

so i thought again
and it occurred to me
maybe i shouldn't write
at all
but clean my gun
and check my kerosene supply

perhaps these are not poetic
times
at all

LAWRENCE BENFORD, born in 1946 in Texas, attended Pan-American College at Edinburg, Texas, majoring in English and Philosophy. His poetry appears in *American Bard* and *The New Black Poetry.*

THE BEGINNING OF A LONG POEM ON WHY I BURNED THE CITY

My city slept
Through my growing up in hate
Bubbling in the back streets.
The sun shone on my city

But curved not its rays back
Into the corners where I shined shoes
With my teeth,
Where my father ate the trash of my city
With his hands,
Where my mother cared for white babies
With black breasts.
My city, yes, outstretched along
Its white freeways slept
In the warmth of its tall new building
And 1000000 $ homes
Of abnormal sapiens with titles

       —And I grew up!

Like a wild beast awaking
To find his mate eaten
In one second I grew up
With the fires that flamed
In my soul. Fires that burned
Holes in the soft spots of my heart.
(So as not to bleed to death)
They were plugged with lead
And I went off to college
With a Gasoline can.

YUSEF IMAN is a young singer, actor, and poet who has been active in LeRoi Jones's *Spirit House.* He can be heard reading poetry on the Jihad Production recording, *Black and Beautiful.*

LOVE YOUR ENEMY

Brought here in slave ships and pitched over board.
Love your enemy.
Language taken away, culture taken away.

Love your enemy.
Work from sun up to sun down.
Love your enemy.
Work for no pay.
Love your enemy.
Last hired, first fired.
Love your enemy.
Rape your mother.
Love your enemy.
Lynch your father.
Love your enemy.
Bomb your churches.
Love your enemy.
Kill your children.
Love your enemy.
Force to fight his wars.
Love your enemy.
Pay the highest rent.
Love your enemy.
Sell you rotten foods.
Love your enemy.
Sell dope to your children.
Love your enemy.
Forced to live in the slums.
Love your enemy.
Dilapidated schools.
Love your enemy.
Puts you in jail.
Love your enemy.
Bitten by dogs.
Love your enemy.
Water hose you down.
Love your enemy.
          Love.
          Love.

Love.
Love.
Love.
Love, for everybody else.
But when will we love ourselves?

VICTOR HERNANDEZ CRUZ, born in 1949 in Aguas Buenas, Puerto Rico, grew up in New York City. His poems have appeared in many leading avant-garde publications and he has a book entitled *Snaps* (1969).

TODAY IS A DAY OF GREAT JOY

when they stop poems
in the mail & clap
their hands & dance to
them
when women become pregnant
by the side of poems
the strongest sounds making
the river go along

it is a great day

as poems fall down to
movie crowds in restaurants
in bars

when poems start to
knock down walls to
choke politicians
when poems scream &
begin to break the air

that is the time of

true poets   that is
the time of greatness

a true poet aiming
poems & watching things
fall to the ground

it is a great day.